DIVINE DAUGHTERS

I am a

am   a   full   wo - man,   I   a

DIVINE DAUGHTERS

LIBERATING THE POWER AND PASSION
OF WOMEN'S VOICES

a   full   wo-man, I   am a

Rachel L. Bagby

to Carol
in Divine Daughterhood
♥
tb
June 2000

HarperSanFrancisco
A Division of HarperCollins*Publishers*

HarperSanFrancisco and the author, in association with The Basic Foundation, a not-for-profit organization whose primary mission is reforestation, will facilitate the planting of two trees for every one tree used in the manufacture of this book.

The author gratefully acknowledges the following: "Vow," was originally published in *Feminist Studies*. A slightly different version of "Tree-Leaf Woman's Song," translated by Miranda Shaw, is in *Passionate Enlightenment: Women and Tantric Buddhism in India*, by Miranda Shaw, Princeton University Press, copyright 1994. Used by permission. Excerpts from Coleman Barks's translation of Rumi are from *The Essential Rumi*, HarperSanFrancisco, copyright 1997. Originally published by Threshold Books, 139 Main Street, Brattleboro, VT 05301. Used by permission.

HarperCollins Web Site: http://www.harpercollins.com
HarperCollins®, ✦®, HarperSanFrancisco™ , and A TREE CLAUSE BOOK® are trademarks of HarperCollins Publishers, Inc.
HarperCollins books may be purchased for educational, business, or sales promotional use. For information please write: Special Markets Department, HarperCollins Publishers, Inc., 10 East 53rd Street, New York, NY 10022.

BOOK DESIGN AND TYPESETTING BY JAIME ROBLES

FIRST EDITION
Library of Congress Cataloging-in-Publication Data
Bagby, Rachel.
Divine daughters: liberating the power and passion of women's voices / Rachel Bagby.
ISBN 0–06–251426–1 (cloth)
ISBN 0–06–251427-X (pbk.)
1. Bagby, Rachel. 2. Afro-American women—Biography. 3. Bagby, Rachel—Family.
4. Daughters—United States—Biography. 5. Philadelphia (Pa.)—Biography. I. Title.
E185.97.B14A3   1999
973'.0496073'0922—dc21   98-45046

99 00 01 02 03 HADD 10 9 8 7 6 5 4 3 2 1

For my mother, father, brother, and husband—
four great teachers of love's transformative powers.

For all daughters.
May we all be free.

CONTENTS

When Must We Sing?

How Does Life Sing Us?

Who dares and who bet' not sing?
(That's bet' as in bet[ter] not, as in my
native Mommatongue and Daddytongue.)
What we obeys which them that bids us
hush? Who then dares help us sing free?
How? When? Where? Why?

Where does the unsung go? Does she die?

Excerpt from "Full Woman,"
written by Rachel Bagby. Copyright
1987 Breathing Music ASCAP. Used
by permission.

missing
the missing members
of our hallowed families

        kin of blessed
        mothers, holy
        fathers, sacred
        sons

whose tongues
have been unheard

whose names
have been unsung

for thousands
for thousands of years

divine daughters

how were you so well hidden
from us for so long?

how are we hidden
from ourselves?

once we have heard
just once
deeply heard your names
interior elder sisters
just once heard all daughters
hold all the people
there will ever be
inside
before ever breathing a breath
being pinked out
learning to be tasty
and everything nice

divine daughters
life will for us be different

DIVINE DAUGHTER SISTERS: AN INVITATION

Enter these pages with the ears of one ready to hear deeply and be deeply heard.

Your voices are my voices.

A Cheyenne proverb says that a people is not broken until the hearts of the women are on the ground. I say our species won't be healthy until the hearts of the daughters are nourished and sound.

Hear, within these pages, song and story cycles of daughters' divine: births-lives-deaths-rebirths-lives. Hear here chants of our lifetimes, sorrow songs and freedom songs, spirituals, praisesongs, and bawdy ballads. Listen, look deeply within these pages for daughters' ways of coming to power-filled terms with interior suns.

Divine daughter sisters, your voices are my voices.

We reach each daughter's soul only by voice, by ear, by heart, and by our singing what we know—bone deep—to be true.

Ours are the voices now becoming skilled in telling *all* who claim to love us: Show your love by listening deeply.

Hear us.

Gather near and lend us your hearts' middle ears.

Our daughterly living and learning accompanies Life's voices. We call and Life responds to our yearnings to be free.

Hear here our dances with the many times and places that require savvy silences. Hear here the places and the ears receptive to our roars.

Hear, within these pages, the polyrhythmic choruses of miracles igniting our upbringings into coming 'rounds of lit living.

Your voices are my voices.

Your voices are my voices, divine daughter sisters.

Listen.

BRINGINGS UP AND COMINGS 'ROUND:
Daughters' Songs

I.

I am a drummer's daughter

daughter of pounding
daughter of sound
of dancing

I am
a child of music
child of movement

She
who
has
learned
to
be
quiet

and still

II.

I am a farmer's daughter

daughter
of daughter
of daughter
of women
who
knew
what to plant
during which growing moon

I am a grandchild
of harpist

music of growing things

III.

I am a many skinned
mixed blood

African, not.

Cherokee
Scottish
East Indian

daughter
of mountains
of hot springs

Which one
is my tribe?

She
who
is
five tribes
in one

IV.

I am death's daughter

child
of the image

of cities

She
who
acknowledges
shadows

daughter
of thistime

I am
of present, of past

She
who
lives
now
what is
coming

V.

I am all daughters

all someday mothers
of daughters
of sons

music
of growing things

still

darkness and colors

of theretime
in heretime

We
who
create
what is
coming

BRINGING OUR VOICES TO LIFE

"**D**OIN' THE BEST I CAN," the first chant to which I gave birth, popped out effortlessly one crisp fall morning on my walk to Stanford Law School from Crothers Hall, the law students' dormitory. It was a work song. In my inner ear, a hand-clapping, foot-stomping community accompanied me. An internal chorus of voices, improvising parts, recreated the rowdily reverent sing-alongs of my youthful rides in the back of the bus on the way to A.M.E. church conferences. The sonic company and hills the color of Momma's skin helped me endure the law school's deafening silences about the strengths and challenges of communities like the one from which I came.

The chant enjoyed an immaculate conception, with no distance to sing of between its genesis and its life in the air. Its 4/4 rhythm, marked out by each step I took, held me steady on the path. "Doin'" sprang spontaneously to my lips as if in answer to an unconscious prayer for sonorous solace on my daily pilgrimage of few external steps but many internal struggles toward becoming a lawyer.

The year was 1977. That year a former KKK member was convicted for the murder of Addie May Collins, Denise McNair, Carole Robertson, and Cynthia Wesley, four young daughters killed in the bombing of the Sixteenth Street Baptist Church in Birmingham, Alabama, in 1963.

In 1977, Dr. Pauli Murray became the first African American female priest ordained by the Episcopal Church in the U.S. Women voted for the first time in Liechtenstein. Mothers in Argentina held the first Rally for the Disappeared in Buenos Aires. African

American artist Ntozake Shange received a Tony Award for her play *for colored girls who have considered suicide/when the rainbow is enuf.*

In 1977, I was a first-year law student at Stanford, one of thirty-five women and seven Blacks in a class of 172. I was the first in my Mommaline to attend law school. That fall was my first in California. I chose to attend Stanford as much for the state in which it stands as for the fact that the law school was ranked one of the top five in the United States. Besides, trees lived in the library. The presence of tall green beings reassured me that I would at least be able to breathe in the windowless carrel I anticipated occupying for 50 percent of my waking hours over the next three years.

The law school's environmental club sponsored a camping trip to Yosemite the weekend following our first week of classes. Only five or six of us decided we could afford to take that much time away from our studies. California was suffering through one of its cyclical, severe droughts. As a consequence, many of Yosemite's reputedly breath-snatching waterfalls were bone dry. I was disappointed to hear variations of "you should've seen this waterfall last year" over and over as we walked past or to the edge of unfathomably large boulders piercing the air like asymmetric lingams erected in praise of Shiva.

Annoyance yielded to a queasy gratitude when our trail leader turned around to tell us that we were lost and that a nearby sans-water rockfall plummeting down to our left led to a trail she was sure would lead us back to camp before dark. Our choices were to shimmy down water-forsaken rocks during the bit of light left or find ourselves in the hard place of being lost in Yosemite at night. (Lions and tigers and bears, oh, my!)

What choice? Shimmy we did, forty-five minutes' worth, down 'sposed-to-be-wet rock. My tent mate and I, both first-time campers, stayed within whispering distance of each other as we made our way down, our butts warmed by what felt like miles of near verticality. As tent mates and trail buddies, we were responsible for each other's safety. She was vociferously afraid of heights. My own fear was lulled by my minute-to-minute reassurances of us both. I chanted, "It's okay, we're doin' fine, we're gonna be all right," until we firmly planted our feet on level ground.

We both survived our sojourn uninjured, though a part of me was claimed by the warm danger of that land. Yosemite initiated me into a deeper relationship with Life. Right then and there, in that place of cliffs the color of my Momma's skin, a place that sustains sequoia, mixed conifers, and manzanita groves, I began to give my voice to Life.

To the wild I returned whenever law school threatened to get on my last nerve. I went to Foothills Park in Palo Alto as often as possible. I particularly enjoyed taking vigorous walks along the serpentine trail, dense with pine, bay laurel, and a seemingly infinite variety of mosses. A portal of bay laurel trunks arched over the trail a few feet from its mouth. Womb and cathedral, this archway exuded a natural incense in which I would linger for a timeless time until the sounds of approaching hikers snatched me back from my reverie.

This trail introduced me to the shy curiosity of fawns. The soprano essential oil of pine and bay laurel released when the forest sunned after a rain or dense fog vigorously evacuated my chronically congested sinuses. This trail was a medicine trail. This trail was one of my teachers, revealing the skin-friendly habitats of mosses, the ability of trees to continue living after toppling over, the security enjoyed by shallow roots that ride out both quaking earth and eroding soil.

Back on campus, I silenced first-year-law-student anxieties by regularly chanting "Doin' the best I can" on the five-minute walk to school in the mornings.

During orientation, Stanford Law's class of 1980 was told we were the crème de la crème, destined to rule the country, if not the world. We were told that our minds and spirits would be sorely tested as our professors prepared us to fulfill our roles. We were lightheartedly forewarned about the possibility of enduring nervous breakdowns and were encouraged to avail ourselves of the counseling services included in our health fees. We were told that we'd have to read so much our sight would probably suffer. We were told to take time off and have fun but not too much time or too much fun.

Institutionally sanctioned and subsidized opportunities for recreation offered alcohol, competitive sporting events, and a yearly trot up a challenging hill to Zotts, a beer garden in a nearby forest. I'd never even heard of a beer garden before, and only now, after years of being a serious herbal apprentice, do I wonder about the genesis of the name. Do traditional beer gardens grow hops?

I found most of the recreational options offered by the school less than nourishing. When the rampant elitism apparent everywhere in this elite law school (what did I expect?) took a liking to my next-to-last nerve, I'd slip into the stairwell and chant echoing rounds of:

> Go down Moses
> Way down in Egypt land
> Tell old Pharaoh
> Let my people go.

Fast-forward to New Year's Eve, December 31, 1981. I am twenty-five years old and standing at the sink in my Momma's house, washing the dinner dishes. What was to have been a semester-long leave of absence from Stanford Law School has stretched out into an entire year. Months earlier, I rode a Greyhound bus across country from California, proud that I earned the money to pay my own way back to my Momma's house.

I went back to my childhood home to begin my life anew. I went back because every other time I turned around in California some pitiful or lustful or shameful or hate-filled white man grabbed at my body or soul, and I felt helpless to stop them.

I went back to my Momma's house to get the stories of the women in my family. Something I musta left in Philadelphia made me dangerously vulnerable. I went back to Momma's house to fetch what was missing, to begin my life again.

Compared to the redwood forests I have come to love, Momma's house feels more like sandpaper on skin than it feels like home. Still, it is the closest thing to home I have. At least I am safe there.

Dad kicked his nasty substance habits—heroin, alcohol, to-bacco—years ago. He is gentle with me. He shows me pictures of happy times our family enjoyed during my childhood. My older brother, Nelson, is so busy teaching music, producing plays, and di-recting church choirs that he is rarely home. It is a joy to finally have the piano to myself for hours and hours. I am old and wise enough to challenge Momma's beliefs without getting hit. Through all our differences, mistakes, and misunderstandings, I know Momma and Daddy and Nelson will care for me in a way that is required to save my life.

It is New Year's Eve, December 31, 1981. I am in my Momma's kitchen, washing dinner dishes. Momma and Dad both come in and invite me to go to church with them for candlelight service. I decline. The only time I feel a sense of true peace in that house is when both of them leave. I miss the silence of forests. I want to be alone. I don't want to be alone. Here I am, twenty-five years old and washing dishes in my Momma's kitchen, a sentence I and not my brother had to bear since childhood because I was the girl.

It is 1981, my older brother has never lived anywhere else but in Momma's house, and I wonder if he has ever washed a single dinner dish. I am remembering Momma telling me that when she dies, "You go'n' have to take care of these men," and my telling her she'd better start training them now to care and cook for themselves 'cause I wasn't going to do it.

I must begin again. I am washing the dishes and wondering about the uses of Momma's knives. I am thinking that if dodging grabby white men or washing dishes in my Momma's kitchen on New Year's Eve is all I have to look forward to, then what's the use of continuing to live?

All I know is that I want out, out of my boxed-in life. I look outside my Momma's kitchen window at the small patch of frozen dirt that will be lush with food and flowers next growing season. The yard is surrounded by chain-link fence on three sides. Barbed wire spirals around the top of the fence to keep burglars out. The yard scene looks like a scaled-down version of those surrounding prisons I've worked in. I've got to get out of here.

"Why not?" I ask, caressing a chef's knife. An Ellingtonian big band responds, horns ascendant. The bassman's fingers are Lindy Hopping all ova his strings. A voice blending the gifts of Ella Fitzgerald, Betty Carter, Abbey Lincoln, and Diane Reeves leaps in, singing:

What a mir-a-cle We_live____ We got So much-a life to share_

So much-a love to give__ And the The joy of laugh-ter song work and play____ I say

What a bless-ing is to-day yeah, yeah, What a mir-a-cle We_ live__

We got So much - a life to share__ So much-a love to give__ And the

The joy of laugh - ter song work and play__ I say Thank you__ thank__

__ you thank you Thank you__ thank__ you for__ to - day.

Excerpt from "Gratitude,"
written by Rachel Bagby. Copyright
1982 Breathing Music ASCAP.
Used by permission.

With chant and bebop, plea and persuasion, some mysterious you-name-this-NON-it heard my call and responded in an irresistibly syncopated YES-CAN-GO-DO-LIVE!

I do not know what to call what answered me. Grandmothering is what I now sometimes call the answering. I am grateful for the answering I no longer feel the need to completely comprehend.

Fast-forward again. It is now nine years later: New Year's Eve, 1990, and I gather with Bobby McFerrin and other members of Voicestra, his ten-member a capella vocal orchestra, in San Francisco's renowned Grace Cathedral. An Anglican church, a treasure-house of marble and stained-glass windows, hostess to the Dalai Lama and a yearly women's spirituality weekend, site of a soul-nourishing labyrinth—Grace Cathedral is the grand dame of Christian monuments in the San Francisco Bay Area and the third largest cathedral in the United States. Its acoustics are legendary.

We Stras, a nickname for Voicestra, gather at Grace Cathedral to sing a dream to life; Bobby's dream of chanting in the new year. The program is entitled, "Singing for Your Life—A 24-Hour Meditation for Healing." From 6 P.M. December 30 to 6 P.M. December 31, Bobby and the Stras take turns directing two-hour periods of vocal music. Individual singers, choirs, extended family members, Stra fans, and the community at large have been called to Grace to sing, to listen, to make a peaceful transition from one year to the next.

"This is not a concert," the invitation says. Anointing and laying-on-of-hands are offered during a trinity of two-hour sessions. Counseling is available around the clock. Along with Bobby and a few other Stras, I have committed to staying in Grace for the entire program. I have come prepared to stay in comfort and wear a woolen shawl-blanket woven by a dear friend, Norma Cordell. My rations include brown rice, a few baked sweet potatoes, lozenges, and a slender thermos of throat-coat tea.

I plan to participate in each two-hour period by taking a twenty-minute nap as needed in a room where the priests normally don their robes of office each Sunday. A woman friend studying to be an Anglican priest is visually and vocally perturbed when I show her my temporary nest. Sleeping on the floor in this room is clearly im-proper behavior in Anglican culture. But ours is an exceptional pro-gram. My humble resting place is not disturbed by any of the legion of priests and church officials present throughout the night.

Nor does anyone offer me more comfortable accommodations. People move in and out. The many conversations, though seemingly endless, are quiet. I pray a prayer of gratitude for the reserved man-ner in which Anglicans usually conduct their conversations. The floor is stone and cold. For this, too, I am grateful. I need to be com-fortable enough to get some rest but not so comfortable that I'll sleep through an entire section of singing.

The group of singers I am to conduct includes Felicia Ward, the woman who alerted me to Bobby's master class at Omega Institute two years earlier. My journey toward becoming a Stra was accelerated in that class. Moments before my two-hour vocal ministry at Grace Cathedral begins, I thank Felicia for her hand in my destiny. She offers me a basket packed with sweet potatoes and thanks me for personally inviting her to join me in singing for our lives.

My group includes several members of VoMo, the Oakland Youth Chorus's talented tenth: kick-butt dancers, singers, and vocal percussionists. I have asked rhythmically gifted singers to join me out of respect for the frequently demanding percussive requirements of the music that calls me its own. I have asked women who love women to be present because of the power of music I've experienced in the presence of well-loved and loving wombed ones. Joey Blake, the bass Stra I can listen to forever, joins us, as does Vicki Randle, who later became a regular on Jay Leno's television show. I stand before these members of what will soon be a sonorous community and pray to help bring forth singing capable of nourishing all of our souls. I pray that the spirits of the singers and the spirits of the listeners and the spirit of what is to be sung will benefit all beings.

Then I listen.

Yemaya, a Yoruba goddess of salt water, emerges in the midst of chaos. Before her arrival all that I heard was a cacophony of rhythms that I tried to make sense of by giving them bodies, lungs, low and high voices.

The women start the call, *Ya-Ya-Yemaya, Ya-Ya-Yemaya.* The men answer *Yemaya ya, Yemaya ya.* Yemaya jumps in $3/4$ time, a trinity to the $4/4$ rhythmic base previously established. Syncopation reigns. The women's voices lead, the men's voices answer, a second women's part harmonizes with the first, then a third, melodic, women's part adds yet another rhythm to our praisesong, *Yema-e-ya e-ya.* The third part, with its swelling *e-ya,* ushers in Yemaya's lulling tongue. The nave of the cathedral is bathed in Yemaya's rhythms, as are the singers.

Excerpt from "Yemaya," written by Rachel Bagby. Copyright 1990 Breathing Music ASCAP. Used by permission.

It is New Year's Eve, 1990, nine years after the New Year's Eve when I declined my parents' invitation to accompany them to candlelight service at church. Nine years later I revel in candlelight in a grand cathedral. I linger in a sonic baptism of Yemaya's salty waters. Here, in a Christian cathedral, I lead twenty singers in a praisesong of Yemaya, a Yoruba goddess. Our voices evoke her grandmotherly comfort.

I lead? I follow Yemaya's call in my ear and spread it around. She calls lullabies out of several of the singers present. A high voice breaks out of the communal lull to cry *Yemaya!* Joey, the bass man, moans a dark chocolate flourish here and there, as if responding to Yemaya's caress.

She is out but not out of place in Grace Cathedral. She is mellifluous: sounding sweet and smooth. She is lulling our bodies into a sensual peace. Over and over we sing her name. The singers and the sung to are all held in Yemaya's embrace.

You may know the one who claimed us by another name. She is Yemonja in one part of the African Diaspora, Yemaya in another. The crash and lull of her, the range of her dimensions, is clear in her powerful sway over singers and those sung to. The hush that fell over the babies present when we began to chant Yemaya's name now seems to blanket us all. Pictures spring into mind with our singing, turquoise oceans, abundant waves; feelings of generosity, a call to sweet release—and enough trust to surrender to the call—accompany giving our tongues to Yemaya.

Bobby's invitation read, "Singing for Your Life—A 24-Hour Meditation for Healing." Is the peace evoked by our chanting a healing peace? Yemaya seems to rock all beings in Grace Cathedral into an audible relaxation response. Medical researchers now claim that spending twenty minutes a day in such a response is essential to the success of integral medical programs in reversing heart disease. As we chant in Grace Cathedral on New Year's Eve, our breaths, tones, intentions, rhythms, and repetitions evoke Yemaya's rolling waters, waters that quiet us into a healing state of being.

Breath. Tone. Intention. Rhythm. Repetition. Every day, the powers designated by these words unite innumerable strangers Earthwide in socially acceptable, sonorous ecstasy. About forty women and a handful of men gather at Gaia Bookstore in Berkeley, California, for my program entitled "Singing Chants of Our LifeTimes." I begin by chanting the essensual elements of chants that have kept me alive: breath, tone, intention, rhythm, and repetition. I chant one word per finger, as I hold up my right hand and chant. *Breath. Tone. Intention. Rhythm. Repetition.* This chant is spoken. I chant it alone two times, then signal the group to join me. Voices join shyly at first, before following my boisterous lead.

I chant, "Breath. Tone." I am silent where the next word would be but hold up the corresponding finger holding its place, and the congregation chants, "Intention." Together, we complete the sequence, "Rhythm. Repetition." We are playing with words. We are learning. I punctuate our repetitions with examples of the places in our everyday worlds pervaded by chant.

Remember the chants from your high-school football games:

B-E A-G-G-R-E-S-S-I-V-E.
Be aggressive, Be aggressive.

Remember the chants generated by Madison Avenue, the chants we call jingles. Millions of dollars are spent daily broadcasting radio and television advertisements created around verbally and musically memorable phrases: jingles. Other fortunes are spent studying which rhythms and number of repetitions anchor jingles in our nervous systems. By their fruits shall we know the intentions behind advertisers' enormous investments in jingles: brand-name recognition and loyalty and the insatiable craving to buy, buy, buy.

I ask the people gathered to create more restorative chants with me. I ask them if there is some word or phrase calling to be amplified in our collective lives. A woman calls out, "When I dance, the universe dances."

"Is that true?" I ask.

"Yes," she says, "yes."

"Great. Does anybody hear anything we can sing to this?" I ask.

Barbara Borden, a drummer and dear friend, says she hears a rhythm, which she starts playing on a talking drum. She and I start whispering the words, *when I dance, the universe dances,* to the rhythms she drums. It is now easy to cue the congregation to begin chanting these words in time, because we are already used to chanting *breath, tone, intention, rhythm, repetition* together, just so. We have three of our elements going strong: intention, rhythm, and repetition. Add a bit more breath, enough to sustain each word being sung on an extended tone, and we now have what I call the floor of a chant, which we sing, again and again and again.

I call out, "Harmonies!"

And instantly harmonies leap out of several mouths, proof positive that they were already there in the singers' ears, waiting to be welcomed. We sing and sing. I add a syncopated line, practicing what I'm preaching: sing what you hear, sing what you hear, sing what you hear. This joyful noise lasts for over three minutes before the chant tells me to bring us to a quiet close. The whole time I'm dancing as we're singing and amazed that nobody else gets up.

"How could you all sing about the universe dancing and not dance?" I ask, dumbfounded.

"We were waiting for permission," a woman responds.

Life gives all gathered the needed permission.

I ask again if anyone has some word or phrase calling for amplification. There are an infinite number of other ways to ask the essential question behind my call for a word or phrase:

*What are you ready to celebrate, over and over, aloud
and with others?*

*Of Life's many blessings, which ones evoke in you the urge
to make joyful noise?*

*Name the qualities, attitudes, and ways of speaking that deeply
nourish your soul.*

For whom, for which forms of Life's generosity, do you speak?

*What do you need to release to align your life with Life's
restorative impulses?*

How do you give voice to your heart's desires?

What are you ready to receive?

How were you so well hidden from us for so long?

How are we hidden from ourselves?

*Do interior dialogues with your longings echo your
breath-by-breath experience?*

*Which of your formidable restorative powers cries out to
be deeply heard?*

What losses have you yet to completely mourn?

How can our voices amplify your creative vibrancy?

What praisesongs ring forth effortlessly from your cells?

All who answer are women. Their answers and the chants we make of them are as varied as the colors of their eyes, hair, and skin.

"Speaking only the truth," floats around the room in a minor mode; its rhythm evokes Hildegardian chant, as in Hildegard of Bingen. "Having fun, la-la-la," sings us smack-dab back into the middle of childhood. "How long does it take to make a good soup?" is the evening's work song. Vegetables could be chopped to this one, soup stock seasoned, onions and garlic sautéed.

"Heal, little brother. Heal," feels like a sung prayer meeting. My Momma would say this one sounds like home. We're singing in the call-and-response idiom where the basses lead. I'm on the bass line with two or three other multioctave-voiced women. We've gotten comfortable enough chanting together by now that harmonies come out without my asking. While many of the folks in this room are friends from Women's Alliance camps, Voicestra concerts, and Black Women's Health Project retreats, many are strangers to one another. Whether stranger or friend, by the end of the evening we consistently keep in time and in tune with one another. Miracles of miracles.

Someone responds to my call to create yet another chant by requesting one I've already recorded. "Full Woman," a chant my body created as an antidote to my post-rape feelings of infinite emptiness, roars out of the mouths of the women present so strongly that it visibly shakes the men. We are dancing and chanting our fullness in a community-based bookstore and cultural institution named Gaia, a goddess-name for Earth. The dancers no longer wait for permission to dance. We're stomping our power and singing in rounds. Harmonies come and go on their own. When our collective beings seem to radiate the fullness we chant ourselves as being, we quiet down into a communal hum. The hush that follows is filled with the ahs and umms of well-fed women.

How does life sing us? Let us live the ways.

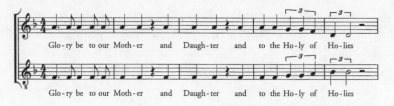

GLORY BE

VOICESTRA'S TONAL CHANTING fed a sonic hunger deep, deep
within my bones. Our wordless singing was filled with stories that sounded more like home than those of many human
communities to which I've belonged. These were the songs the forests
sang, these were the offspring of the ringing IS, everywhere alive, that
showed no preference for daughters or for sons. Even before I joined
Voicestra, tonal chants frequently came into my ears; unbidden. They
raised themselves all up into my chest with a force I could not resist.
Life's moaning songs and glory singing, springing out of my mouth,
often attracted other critters as accompanists and audience: seagulls
creating a circle of sound above me as I sang with the ocean; catties
circumambulating my legs around the house.

In the wild, I'd marvel at the synchronicity of the birdsong or seal
bellow that sounded like response to my singing. I was astonished to
learn, years later, of musicians actually making small fortunes with
such play.

Indoors, I would hush when the critters gathered 'round my feet as I sang. Perhaps some overcivilized part of me was embarrassed that my singing attracted the attentions of other animals. Or I thought my singing bothered them, forgetting that the one cat who always came and purred by me while I sang would reliably use her claws to tell me when I did something she didn't like.

Chanting in circle with Voicestra, dancing to Bobby's improvs, I was that cat. More precisely, my entire being felt like a cat's purr sounds. The sound of Life's tongue in my ears felt kinesthetically related to the chants that sprang out of Bobby's mouth and were passed to each Stra, as if each chant were an elixir from the long-sought fountain of infinity, where neither youth nor age nor death held any meaning.

Bobby gives each section of Voicestra a part made up of rhythmically repeated syllables. Our voices become both the fingers and singing skins essential to communal drumming at a village gathering. As we chant, I hear an unworded story of planting and harvest, a story my body must dance. In the midst of chanting my part, "wayOhloAh," in response to the altos' call, I vibe Bobby the message, I have to dance to this story, Bobby, I have to dance.

He hears me, though I've not said a word. Bobby comes up behind me and says, "Go do something." Gently, he takes my microphone and says, "Go do something, dancewise."

Slowly, I move into center stage and surrender each breath, each cell, each impulse of volition to the story my body hears in the rhythms Voicestra chants. My knees and back bend forward until the latter is parallel to the stage and is undulating the story close to the floor. The wooden planks beneath me become rows newly prepared to receive seeds. These I plant, not knowing what the crops will be but knowing that they will be. I plant.

And Bobby chants, "She's planting our food, she's planting our food."

My breasts pulse toward the stage constantly as I next outline a round, wide, invisible basket with my left arm, a basket into which I dance the crops I harvest from the newly planted field, and Bobby chants, "She gathers the food, she gathers the food."

Now, up, my breasts are up and pulsing toward the audience, to whom I offer the first fruits of the harvest before turning to feed my sistah and fellow Stras. As Bobby chants, "She's sharing the food," he moves toward me with my mike and I return to being an indistinguishable voice in the choir, another "wayOhloAh," no longer sharing the full-body picture translations of our chant, although I continue to feel and internally dance them.

The sonic and visual sustenance pulls the audience to its feet. They join their voices to ours and continue singing after we've moved off the stage, gathered in our circle of chanting backstage, turned off our mikes, and received the stage manager's reminder that we are renting our ritual space. She prods us to get out of there before the unions start charging us double time and a half for exceeding our contracted time.

We disregard the on-and-on calling of our spirits to dance, to chant. We hush. We disregard the spirits of our still-singing audience. The chant yearns to be sung, yet we dampen our engagement in life-giving and -given rhythms. We learn, for the sake of the measurable and measured, to act quiet and feign being still.

We shut our mouths.

But our closed lips do not *(cannot!)* stop the singing. We dance down the stairs; the chanting rings in our ears, masquerading as jabbering laughter. We hug, kiss, move into hers and his dressing rooms. Snatches of chanting, naked as we are sans costumes, escape our lips as we liberate grateful feet from torturously pointy-toed shoes.

Our bodies become the chanting that fills the stairwell as we sashay out to the van waiting to carry us off to our hotel.

I tremble, haunted by the sensual nourishment of becoming the sung. By singing Life's songs I am also sung into being. My cells echo the Native American Keres' stories of Nau'ts'ity and Ic'sts'ity—divine daughter sisters who are sung into being and who sing into being all that is. I long for my external skin to be loved as unreasonably and well as the sung's interior lovers: diaphragm, each lobe of my left and right lung, larynx, tongue, upper and lower lips, and each of my body's hungrily listening cells.

I was lonely for in-the-flesh company in embodying the Life-affirming sung: nourishing singing, sonorous soul-food. I tasted such singing in church, but there it was usually tainted by the aftertaste of privileged fathers or sons or mere ghosts where daughters or mothers would otherwise, naturally, relationally be. Each of my pre-Voicestra vocal communities fell short of satisfying my sonic hunger.

These earlier vocal communities came together to cheer on athletes engaged in cutthroat sports: *B-E A-G-G-R-E-S-S-I-V-E. Be aggressive. Be aggressive.* Or we combined our breaths to pledge allegiance to a flag and republic where hardly anybody was *really* free, or to sing in choirs directed by folks who apparently deemed our voices unworthy of compositions by non-Europeans. In Black vocal communities of spirit and social engagement, we most often lifted up the holy, only males of patriarchal religions. In women's groups gathered to celebrate the seasons of our activism, our sung praises of goddesses bore Sumerian, Greek, or Roman names, so many of which felt foreign on my tongue. And gatherings to sing our thanksgivings to Life and an Earthma (we must take care of) for fortifying us in our day-to-day actions toward creating just and restorative cultures were all too infrequent.

But the Stras' tonal chanting coaxed stories out of my cells. The rhythms of our singing helped my spine remember that planting growing things had a Life-sustaining cadence, gathering nourishment could be sweet, and the bounty could be freely shared and sung with both stranger and family.

An unbiased generosity characterized the vocal communities constructed out of air thick with Voicestra's improvised chanting. The promise of arriving in the home we made with voice, with breathing sounds, made it easier to endure the Stras' squabbles about the other parts of our show: who got to solo, whose compositions would be sung, which one of the sopranos was too flat or sharp or diffuse or blaring or not blending in. I was a prime offender. But when I wholeheartedly lent Life my tongue in vocal community, the oddly gnawing, unnamed hungers, fed by being deemed culturally unholy, momentarily quieted themselves in my soul.

For, you see, my skin, gender, and preference for the unworded sung often earned me the treatment of someone in need of redemption or assimilation. In other words, *if* I disowned the earth-hued beauty of my Mommatongue in favor of speaking, thinking, and singing in so-called standard English (or Italian or Latin or German or French) *and* I emulated male spiritual masters—practiced the teachings of the Buddha or personally accepted Jesus' saving grace— *or* adopted the beliefs and memorized chants from Americanized versions of resurrected Goddess religions, *then* I might have some hope of being okay.

Even in Voicestra, when we sang worded praisesongs about spirit, we anthropomorphized divinity, using the dominant culture's conventional pronoun for human: *he.*

The shes outnumbered the hes in Voicestra. We were six women and four men. Our joy and mission were to express the full range of our voices' powers, to become a vocal orchestra capable of realizing Bobby's sonic visions, sounding now like a red hot rhythm section, now like a summer rain, now like driving horns backing up an outrageous improvisation of a jazz classic, now like a village celebrating the harvest.

In the beginning, Voicestra rehearsed three mornings a week in a church in San Francisco's Diamond Heights district. We usually learned and rehearsed our parts in a circle, sopranos to Bobby's left, then circling 'round to altos and tenors, and ending with basses on Bobby's right. There were three people on each of the women's parts, two on the men's. One day, after rehearsing one of several gospel songs in our repertoire, Rhiannon, a powerhouse of an alto, teacher, and elder in women's music circles, asked, "How come in all the spiritual songs we sing, we praise a him?"

A familiar energy of *oh-oh* whipped around the circle in anticipation of a heated debate. Rhiannon's question was courageous, given Bobby's very public and frequent articulation of devout Christianity. True to his spirit of creative collaboration with the Stras, Bobby asked Rhiannon to say more. She talked about the many cultures that recognize the divine in female form. She talked about wanting that diversity to live on our tongues.

Bobby showed up at the next rehearsal with a newly composed musical interpretation of the Twenty-Third Psalm. "The Lord is my shepherd. I have all I need. . . ." Its simple, Gregorian chant–like melodic structure contained a lyric innovation that the Gregory after whom Gregorian chant is named would certainly have considered radical: "Beside the still waters *she* shall lead. She restores my soul, she rights my wrongs. . . ."

Throughout most of our first sight-singing of the piece, I kept one eye on the music and the other on the Stras whom I thought might consider it a sacrilege to articulate God as She. We snatched glances at one another; eyebrows raised, eyes widened. But when we came to the lines, "Glory be to our Mother, and Daughter, and to the Holy of Holies," my vision was clouded by tears.

I was barely able to complete the song. The notes had difficulty making it past what felt like a rainforest in my throat. Seven simple words, "Glory be to our Mother and Daughter," gave voice to a thirty-three-year-old struggle to find a sense of divinity in daughterhood and to heal a spiritually crippling estrangement from my Momma's wisdom practices.

Momma and I rarely discuss anything of import without her bursting into prayer and admonishing me, "Thank God, girl. Pray to God, he will guide you." For years, Momma and I couldn't practice the vocal wisdom traditions of prayer together because in imagery, scripture, and deference to sons, the god who lived on Momma's lips seemed to be the same god given credit for ordaining the actions of violently xenophobic and misogynistic white men.

Discovering that the word *god* is derived from a Latin root translated as "Life Itself" helped Momma and me develop mutually respectful, shared practices and the language with which to communicate our spiritual insights and yearnings.

Singing Bobby's rendition of the Twenty-Third Psalm was the first time that I remember singing a praisesong about daughters' embodiment of Life Itself. Igniting this possibility in a Christian church, the tongue aflame in a sung prayer—a vocal wisdom tradition deeply heard and practiced by folks in my Mommaline—moved me to tears. Mine were not the only moist eyes in our circle that morning.

Upon emerging from the hush enfolding us all at the end of our rehearsal, I asked if Bobby or any of the Stras had ever before heard or sung something praising daughters' luminosity.

Not one of us said yes. And if you were asked that question today, how would you answer?

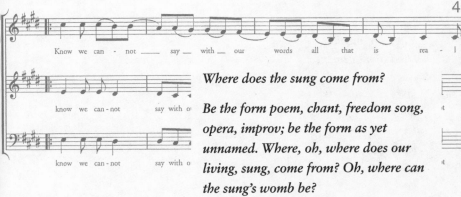

Where does the sung come from?

Be the form poem, chant, freedom song, opera, improv; be the form as yet unnamed. Where, oh, where does our living, sung, come from? Oh, where can the sung's womb be?

Where does the sung come from? How do Life's moans, groans, and sorrow soundings make our breaths its own? How do Life's joys and questions woo our bodies, woo our tongues into freedom singing, freedom claiming our limbs as its home?

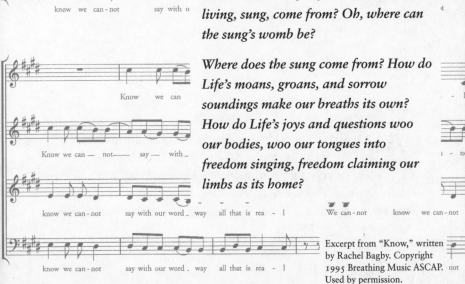

DRUMMER'S DAUGHTER

I.

I am a drummer's daughter

daughter of pounding
daughter of sound
of dancing

I am
a child of music
child of movement

She
who
has
learned
to
be
quiet

and still

A DRUMMER'S DAUGHTER, daughter of pounding, mounts a red, meant-to-be-stationary rocking horse from the side— and fiercely. I am four years old. I mount Horsey as a Petro Loa, a wrathful Vodoun deity, would mount me, her horse—an entranced and dancing devotee—in the midst of a ceremony. But there is no ceremony, no community of devotees surrounding me, protecting me, making sure the honored energy I ride or carry doesn't fry my young behind.

Daddy, a drummer, says I ride Red Horse in anger. Momma says I ride in anger and joy and every day. If I am mad when I get on, I am fine when I get off. Whatever my emotion, Life drums hot in me, hot as Red Horsey is red. I ride, ragefully and joyfully tearing up Momma's walls. In terror, ecstasy, and snot, with tears, questions, and turmoil, embodying both the awful and the wonderfully untame in my Momma's house, I ride a blood red Horsey.

Horsey was built to stand in one place and go back and forth, back and forth. Its base of four sturdy two-by-fours is also dried-blood red. Attached to the wood are metal springs Momma says must weigh thirty pounds each, springs attached to a horse that was built to go back and forth, head down, then butt down, like a seesaw.

My older brother, Nelson, from whom I inherited Horsey, rode it back and forth, back and forth, for years, so gently. But I knew from the way the cowboys rode their horses on TV that if I rode Horsey hard enough, we could both break free from boring stability.

I rear Red Horse so far back that my back, head, and butt almost parallel the floor. I lean so far back that the front of Horsey's foundation rises up. I go almost to the point of being crushed by blood-colored wood, before throwing Horsey's dangerous weight forward, and we leap forward, screeBOOMscreeBOOM.

My four-year-old muscles alone are no match for what I ride against. My hands can't get around Daddy's arms, muscular as they are with drumming and roofing and breaking up dining room furniture.

Now he is my fun Daddy, sitting at the dining room table, talking loud, making up voices for each of the three little pigs and the big bad wolf and the different houses being blown down. Now he is safe.

Now Daddy is dangerous. Now he is drunk and smells nasty. Now I had better be quiet and very still so that he won't get mad and be mean to me. He is raging at Momma and lifting the table up and slamming it back down and breaking it. Now he is high and asleep and pulling on the arm of the chair and yelling at my Momma who has yet to come home from work, Butch, Butch, give me more covers. Now he takes two forevers stumbling up one stair. Now Daddy scares me.

Now Daddy is fun again. He takes me to the zoo, and we eat lots of pink cotton candy. We go to amusement parks and Daddy rides the roller coasters with Nelson while Momma rides with me through the spooky house. Cars filled with my uncles and cousins, aunts and grandparents caravan to the seashore in Wildwood, New Jersey, every summer. Nelson leaps bravely into the freezing water and swims. Momma rushes to save me when I scream as the waves lick my shins.

We play many games as a family—Sorry, Monopoly, Clue, pick-up sticks. I am a poor loser. Daddy loves to remind me of the time we were playing Monopoly and I flew into such a rage about losing that I threw the board, box, pieces and all the money I could get my hands on into the air.

Now Daddy's lying. He's telling Momma he didn't smoke something downstairs that now smells up the whole house. He says somebody threw what we smell into the open cellar window. Momma knows better, and so do I.

Now Daddy lets me sip beer over Momma's objections. Now I sit on his handsome friend Jack's lap and look up into his face and swoon. Oh, Yack, I say—not yet able to pronounce the *J* of his name—I like you. Now Momma and Daddy argue. Their fussing never turns into cussing or fists, but still it is terrible and frequent. It is dark, and their yelling snatches me awake. Daddy barks his refrain, "I'm always wrong, you're always right." I leap out of bed, again, and tell them to shut up, again, so that I can get some sleep.

The warm has left my bed. The cold of beer cans—metal, bent, and sharp—now takes warmth's place. My Daddy's chant, "I'm always wrong, you are always right," takes me over, and my heart now pumps stale beer. Home isn't home. Even though I had my own room, a part of me doesn't feel safe there.

Now Daddy tells me I'm his girl. Now Daddy tells me all the ways that Momma doesn't let him play his drums or run with his musician friends or be the artist he could be, if only. I grow up hearing that Daddy played with Billie Holiday and John Coltrane—geniuses of edges expressed through metal and lips. I grow up thinking it's my fault he didn't make a similarly big name for himself.

"Your Momma held me back," he says. "I was on the road playing, making good money." Money Momma says she never saw. "Your Momma called and said she was pregnant. Told me I'd better stay home or have none." As an adult I learn that Momma made that call when she was pregnant with Nelson. But in my childhood's now, it's Daddy and me and creativity against the world. Now he holds up his intertwined right pointer and index fingers and says, this is you and me, baby, this is you and me.

Now Daddy beats me. He is beating me repeatedly for a crime I didn't commit: his wooden carpenter's ruler was *not* in my hands when it broke. "I didn't do it!" I scream. "Shut up," he says, hitting me.

We played alone a lot, Nelson and I. He, older by four years, would take the lead. We borrowed tools from Daddy's bottom drawer. We practiced building houses in the sky. Dad's wooden ruler, jointed foot by foot, was ladder, spying glass, magician's wand. Then one day, yes, Nelson and I were playing with Daddy's ruler, and, yes, it is broken, but, no, I was not holding it when it snapped, and the beatings won't change that.

We're on round three of Daddy beating first Nelson and then me. He is determined to beat an agreed-upon truth out of us. It's my turn again. I squirm my body down across Daddy's knees. Insisting on my innocence doesn't help. Each lick of his hand is accompanied by a word of his chant, "You bet' not cry, you bet' not cry." I am telling the truth and getting beaten. I am being beaten because my brother lied.

This round over, I stumble out of Nelson's room to announce round four. Down the hall, Nelson stands beside Momma as she sits on her and Daddy's bed. She is stroking Nelson's hand, talking to him softly; seems to be comforting him. I feel helpless and alone. Why isn't anybody doing something soft to or for me? Nothing protects me—not truth, not memory, not crying, not not crying.

Momma and Nelson come to the back room, Nelson's room, the beating room, and Nelson confesses. I turn to Daddy and say, I told you so! He says, That's life. Not Daddy, not Nelson, not Momma ever apologizes. Drowned in my hot tears, some sense of family dies. That's life, Daddy says.

What I hear in that moment: to be beaten for telling the truth is life. To be lied on is life. To be betrayed by your brother and brutalized over a broken ruler by your father while your mother stands by is life. To be helpless is life. To be beaten for playing is life. To have nobody home who believes or protects you is life. To watch your brother be comforted by your mother while you're beaten by your father for telling the truth is life. To have Daddy say and act like he loves you one minute then turn around and hit you and hit you and make you stop crying and yell at you while he hits you like he hates you and acts like it's normal to hurt you and never apologize is life. Violence is life.

I ride the rage of the family. I ride the questions and the pain, ride the unresolved confusion. I grip Red Horsey's handles and pull them back, pull Horsey toward me and then blend with red wood and metal, invite its weight closer, until Horsey and I became a we whose momentum I know intimately and throw forward powerfully: scree-BOOMscreeBOOMscreeBOOM. Rhythmically, with the sound of a work crew pounding tracks, I lean back, leap forward, lean back, thrash forward, lunge through my Momma's house, bound around impossible corners, pounding out rhythms of freedom.

The hallways of Momma's two-story brick house in Philly are only wide enough for one person to pass through at a time and can accommodate some of Momma's more endowed women friends only if they turn sideways. But these hallways are wide enough for me to ride through, rage through, BOOMscreeBLAM (oops) through, from the living room to the kitchen and back and forth and back.

I practice to get good at turning Red Horsey around without dismounting. Bit by bit, leaning first to my right to build up momentum, I then pivot wood and metal to the left, step-by-step, pounding the floor in small arcs to make a turn of 180 degrees. I love making Horsey jump from the living room down the narrow hallway between the stairwell and living room wall, between Momma's dining room chairs and her girl-you-scratch-it-I-kill-you buffet to the doorjamb of the kitchen and back again and again.

Dad says when I ride Red Horsey full out he sees himself in me and it frightens him. Seeing that much foolishness, that much fight, in a girl is enough to scare any grown man, Daddy says. He says I ride Red Horsey in anger. Momma says I ride for fun.

In anger or fun, I just about rode Red Horsey into the ground. At least I didn't intentionally destroy Horsey, as I did many of Nelson's other toys. Off came the wheels to his cars and trains. Into his belly I sank my teeth. Nelson says I started biting him in the stomach as soon as I could reach it. Says the biting only lasted for months until our parents gave him permission to beat me out of the habit. Says he would hear me coming before he felt me. Says that I would come to bite him loud and angry, often crying. The whirling image of a cartoon character, the Tasmanian devil, comes to mind.

I say I rode Horsey in anger and power and all else that made me something other than sugar and spice and every damned-daughter nice. I say Red Horsey's back was where I first practiced riding Life's red, rocky moments, where I first practiced reining in Life-threatening momentum before being crushed.

of dancing

Dancing became an acceptable expression for energies otherwise deemed unladylike for a growing-up girl suddenly too long-legged to ride a worn-out Red Horsey. As soon as I turned five and began school, off came the pants, on went the dresses, revealing constantly scabby knees because I refused to do right like Momma said: "Chile, stop running all high-legged."

But call it a show, put on costumes and makeup, leotards and toe shoes, throw a leg up in the air to Chopin or the tune of an old Broadway musical, and, presto-change-o, the high-strung hussy of a daughter magically becomes a multiply talented child.

Momma pays for me to study classical ballet at Settlement Music School. I study with the physical passion honed on Horsey and become a star in the class. Then I pass the entrance audition to be placed in a master class. I am the only Black child there. My first day turns out to be my last. When the teacher turns her high German accent into my ear and tells me I will never be a real ballet dancer because my butt is too high, something dies inside me. I believe her. Her words become prophecy.

Joy still manages to fill up my sans-ballet young life. Put yourself in this picture. You are a daughter in an extended, rambunctious, familial, poor urban neighborhood. Dance is one of your many Mommas, rhythm your Daddy's right-hand man; your umpteen aunties and uncles are hymns, jump rope, and hand chants, classical music, gospel, jazz, chorales, radio-blasted oohBabyBaby monster hits; and they all demand respect and *rule* you. The drippy kitchen faucet becomes cause to interrupt the dinner dishwashing with a dance routine and improvised chorus that gets you screamed at, "Girl, shut up. I'm watching the football game."

Daddy, in football, what is there to hear? Now, it doesn't matter that in years to come Daddy will spend many hours chauffeuring me to choir rehearsals, attending performances, hauling papers to paper drives to help pay my airfare to Europe with my high school choir, the Ambassadors of Song. Now, all that matters is that, once again, I, *the girl*, am told I have to shut up.

Nelson can be as loud as he pleases, anywhere in the house, any hour of the day or night as long as it's in the service of music. It is not yet 7 A.M., and his playing of the "Thunderbird Suite" snatches me awake after a night's sleep already shortened by my parents' fighting. Every day, whenever Nelson wants to practice, the television comes off. He vetoes football. He never has to clean one thing in the house; he has no daily chores.

Momma says domestic duties are as they are because I am *the girl* and Nelson uses his music to contribute money to the household— has since he began playing for churches at the age of four. Momma says Daddy treats Nelson differently because he hurt Nelson bad once when he was high and he bends over backward ever since to regain his son's love and confidence. Every summer from the age of five through high school, Nelson goes away to music camp in eastern Pennsylvania's Pocono Mountains for an entire month. Our

DRUMMER'S DAUGHTER

godmother endowed his summer musical refuge before she died. She died before I was old enough for her to endow mine. Music is Nelson's life, and my parents' support for his music is unconditional. Momma's house is Nelson's place of respite, rejuvenation, and boundless creativity. Period.

Now, I am told to hush. Stop the singing, stop the activity that makes the inequity of house chores almost pleasant but not resentment free. I am told to stop composing vocal music because my compositions compete with a passive spectator sport blasting on TV. I must shut up so that Daddy can hear as well as see moving pictures of men running around with a ball in their hands, chasing and crashing into one another, and knocking one another down.

I refuse to comply.

Closing my throat to reach high, high notes quietly, I defy my father. Night after night of closing my throat to practice singing without detection, I habitually choke back the brilliance of effortless song. Thirty years later, I am still learning how to sing without a sense of self-strangulation. Thirty years later, my ability to sing relaxed is still impaired. Residual tension limits my ability to consistently sing in full voice.

I am a child of foot-stomping music, child of full-out ecstatic movement and singing allowable in church. Sistahs and brothers caught by spirit *shout,* sing free all over the place. Their praisesongs, "Yes, Lawd," or "JEsusJEsusJEsus" (breath), "JEsusJEsusJEsus" (breath), careen out of their mouths in a cadence that sends all attentive nearby kids running before their elders' sanctified arms start flying all upside somebody's head and before their elders' feet start stomping whatever is unfortunate enough to be underfoot as far to the left and the right as they possibly can stomp and still keep their butts sitting down like all good civilized moved-up-North Negro Christians.

Folks' bodies respond in a spirit eldered by drumming. Ignited by the preacher's message, have mercy, reached by the gospels sung by the youth, yes Lawd, sistahs' and brothers' spines convulse into a song moved-up-North Negroes are normally too sadiddy to sing out loud with each and every cell. Yet folks can't resist the music's irresistible call.

And the red waters now thrashing through their veins were once oceans, blue and lapping the shores of America's eastern edges, were once drumming down on slave ships that brought many of their Mommas' Mommas' Mommas and Daddies here to be bought and sold.

All of this calls me its daughter. Its music and movements, memories and miseries call me into extremes of voice and song and feelings and actions and wonderings and longings I cannot always explain.

she
who
has
learned
to
be
quiet

and still

R HYTHM REQUIRES STILLNESS, requires the absence of
sound. An arrhythmic heartbeat, with its irregular se-
quences of pounding and pauses, is but one of many health
indicators whose measure depends upon stillness. The duration of
unsounded sound between beats determines a rhythm's essential
character. Slow down the most complex polyrhythmic riff, and
you'll find moments of quiet without which all that pulsates, that is
all of Life, ceases to exist.

Being silenced by cultural mandate or commercial intentions is
one thing. Enjoying the privilege of listening deeply within a chosen
quietude for restorative silence is a very profound other.

I love the silence out of which poems sing themselves into my
pen. I love the silence that gives tongue to the body's other senses,
the silence that feeds the finger's ears and nourishes the skin's ability
to know when rain is coming.

I so love silence that I decided to celebrate my thirtieth birthday
in a holy hush. It had long been my habit to spend at least a week a
year in solitary retreat on a Shasta bioregion upland I call Mom
Mountain. Mom Mountain sustained me while I endured and recov-
ered from multiple sexual traumas at the age of twenty-five. Her

power to answer my cries of devastation with restorative beauty drew me back to her year after year.

To prepare for my thirtieth-birthday retreat, I gathered together the women and men closest to my soul and asked them to bring some expression of what they most cherished of themselves that they would love to see amplified in me. I rented a small theater space in Palo Alto, California, where I lived at the time. I needed a large room with several nooks and crannies, a good sound system, room enough for seventeen people to sit comfortably in a circle. That room became a walk-in altar. I adorned one corner with arrangements of my favorite books: dictionaries and volumes of poetry, the collected works of Alice Walker, Toni Morrison, and Rilke. Watercolors, paper, pens and ink, mandalas of music manuscripts and tapes and albums created islands devoted to particular creative mediums, connected by swirls of shawls. The decor was as sinuously polyrhythmic as the music filling the air.

A circle of seventeen candles formed a flickering, ovoid centerpiece around which seventeen friends gathered to wish me well.

We gathered two days before my actual thirtieth birthday. The gift of self that each friend offered me aloud—compassion, crystallized solidity, generosity and focus of gifts, regality of pregnancy and birth, creativity, gentle persistence, beauty in the ordinary, the holy spirit as poetry, outrageousness, groundedness, passion, beauty, art in all of art's forms, hugs and kisses and shells from Hawaii—rode their voices into my ears. With voice, with breathing sound, my friends bathed me in waves of well-wishes. I entered my birthday in silence, walking the broad thighs of Mom Mountain, steeping in my friends' blessings.

My first moontime of my thirtieth year began on my natal retreat. Blessing of blessings! The red times of my menstrual cycle are times of strong dreaming and chanting. Bleeding on moss while walking on Mom Mountain, I prayed to receive a Self-illuminating poem befitting my transition into what I then thought of as old age.

In the silence of my thirtieth birthday, Mom Mountain gave me "Bringings Up and Comings 'Round," the pentad of poems that serves as connective tissue for *Divine Daughters*. All but one of the poems were born whole, complete. Only the centerpiece, *I am a many skinned / mixed blood,* required extensive revisions. I suspect my troubles with getting that poem right had more to do with the social milieu in which it was written than with the poem itself.

The year is 1986. According to a Stanford University study, U.S. women are no better off economically than they were in 1959. The U.S. Supreme Court upholds affirmative action plans to remedy past discrimination on the basis of race, color, and gender. And Linda Brown Buckner, the original plaintiff in *Brown v. Board of Education of Topeka,* reopens the case, contending that the school district had yet to comply with the landmark desegregation ruling of 1954.

The poems of "Bringings Up and Comings 'Round," which I now affectionately refer to as BC, have since served as a kind of midline on the embryonic plate of my existence, a midline around which Life's explorations of identity, equity, and conditioning continue to be sung. The questions that haunt me, the ones I love, as Rilke suggested, for their very own selves, all have homes in BC.

As my fortieth year approached, the fifth poem of BC, *I am all daughters,* challenged me to decipher its deeper truths in my being. I longed to do so in community, silence, and spiritual deepening for an extended time.

In preparation for entering my forties, a decade that often proves to be so pivotal in daughters' lives, I felt the need to cultivate wisdom and compassion. Insight Meditation Society, a Buddhist meditation and retreat center in Barre, Massachusetts, offered the most resonant possibility: a retreat focused on metta (loving-kindness or compassion) practices the first week, followed by vipassana (insight or wisdom) practices the second.

I was introduced to metta and vipassana practices in the heart of the Carson National Forest near Taos, New Mexico. There, in the sweet air conditioned by ancient Ponderosa pines and amid wildly flowered valleys cradling the Vallecitos River, Vallecitos Mountain Refuge offers phone-, fax-, and electricity-free retreats to social and environmental activists.

Quieting our voices amplified the sounds of our breaking and healing hearts.

The vipassana practice of noting fleeting thoughts and emotions made it painfully clear that my breath and interior dialogues were filled with anticipatory adversity. Aha! I thought, this is the combat breath that Franz Fanon referred to: a kind of armored, barely breathing mode of being that people under siege develop and never quite seem to shake. I spent hours fighting the echoes of previously experienced or expected resistance in response to my wants or needs.

I spent precious time in the meditation hall entrapped by the habit of practicing multiple maneuvers, vocal and otherwise, for meeting adversity. *I am hungry. I smell the aroma of freshly baked bread wafting up from the kitchen. I am allergic to wheat, as are many other retreatants. I assume that the baker has not bothered to make a wheat-free version of whatever the others will soon enjoy. Anger arises.*

I imagine organizing a protest rally to articulate the demands of wheat-free people. We don't ask for much: equal pasta, equally fresh bread, equally delicious desserts, edible beauty. Our rallying chant, also simple, "Wheat-free equality. Wheat-free equality," assumes the cadence of my heartbeat. My plans, our demands, the chant momentarily distract me from the pain of anticipating being ne-glected, again.

One upsetting interior episode would barely end before another began.

My husband Martin and I are at a public gathering. Yet another white girl is enthralled by his caramel cuteness. She acts on her at-traction. There, in front of my face, she is rubbing and rubbing all over him. Clear her intentions. Clear his enjoyment of her atten-tions. Clear my anger and eagerness to stop my man from enjoying that woman.

I pull them apart. I yell and scream. I hate myself for acting pos-sessively. I hate feeling as though I am owed an exclusive allegiance of sensual enjoyment from my husband, hate to have my twisted sense of ownership violated, hate facing this evidence that I've inter-nalized the propaganda of being inferior to white girls, hate feeling helplessly diminished by jealousy once again.

I took some solace in the fact that some of the adversarial fan-tasies had larger, social implications.

I fantasize being at a Sweet Honey in the Rock concert, listening to them sing a story that traces a blouse from pesticide-soaked cot-ton fields through several third-world sweatshops, to the sale table from which the singers purchase the tainted item. The women of Sweet Honey are sumptuously dressed in costumes handmade, no doubt, by some woman in the U.S., but where does the fabric come from?

I fantasize being in a room-sized closet stuffed with multiple racks of physically spotless yet politically smelly costumes. I am there with a horde of my artist sistah-friends. I tell them my pledge to only wear secondhand clothing because of what Sweet Honey sings. I want my hands and breasts and limbs to be clean. I tell my friends about the research I've done to substantiate the continuing

damage of the clothing industry, tell them about the Chinese immi-
grant woman and activist who speaks of working so long and inten-
sively on red fabric that she breathes red on her children when she
goes home.

In response to my sung-story about trying to live with integrity in
a world simultaneously shaped by the horrors of apparel manufac-
turing and the financial/cultural rewards of being exquisitely
adorned, my sistah-friends say, "We are not there yet." The fantasy
ends with Sweet Honey singing the title and last line of their song,
"Are My Hands Clean?"

By the end of my retreat at Vallecitos, I felt simultaneously exhausted and cheated, and yet grateful to know that so much of my
attention seemed uncontrollably devoured by combat breathing. I
was also inspired by the moments when I seemed to simply breathe.
I was somehow healed by each breath breathed freely.

Metta, or loving-kindness practice, balanced the often-challeng-
ing insights that arose during vipassana meditations. During metta
meditations we repeated some variation of four phrases: *May I be*
free of danger. May I be happy and peaceful. May I be healthy and
strong. May I live with ease.

We were instructed to direct these phrases first toward ourselves,
then toward a benefactor, someone who has shown us kindness,
generosity, assistance, someone toward whom we feel gratitude.
Next we directed the phrases toward a friend. *May you be free of*
danger. May you be happy and peaceful. May you be healthy and
strong. May you live with ease.

We then directed the phrases, all variations on the theme of well-
wishing, toward a neutral person. Finally, we were encouraged to
bring a difficult person to mind and wish him or her well.

When the retreatants circled at retreat's end to give our voices to
one another as a group for the first time in a week, my offering

began with a wordless song and ended with thanksgiving for all the music that filled me when combat readiness did not.

The Vallecitos retreat inspired me to cultivate freedom from the debilitating habits of combat breathing. I vowed to explore the efficacy of cultivating an interior stillness from which to more skillfully face encounters with adversity. Attending the IMS retreat for my fortieth birthday was one way I intended to make good on my vows.

Both my fortieth birthday and IMS's twentieth anniversary—on St. Valentine's Day, no less!—occurred during the loving-kindness week.

To share the practice of silence and loving-kindness with the 160-some other people gathered at IMS gave me a feeling of joy I can barely describe. I was the only Black woman on the retreat. Yes, I noticed, and I wasn't the only one who did. There were also no Black men on the retreat, though there was one on staff, whom I thrilled to see periodically. Yes, I did *see* this brother, even though retreatants were instructed to avoid eye contact with others as a means of remaining truly focused on our own experience, a means of cultivating an inner silence in the midst of community.

Even as I indulged in peeking behavior, which I deemed a minor violation of retreat guidelines, I loved being in the company of women and men and trusting that no one would bother me, if we kept our fundamental agreement of silence. Our time together seemed designed to protect us from the ordinary challenges of sexual politics. The retreat was led by two women and one man, all of whom are respected teachers and widely read authors of books about Buddhist practices. The man was not in charge. The women were not his subtly-less-powerful colleagues. The teachers' good-natured collaboration was inspiring as they rotated support and leadership roles throughout the retreat.

Our days at IMS were organized into alternating periods of sitting and walking meditation, a midmorning instruction section, an afternoon period of questions and answers, and an evening talk. Every other day we met in small groups of eight to ten practitioners with one of the three instructors. These sessions were called interviews, and they allowed each person time to ask more in-depth questions than those asked in the large-group afternoon sessions. The smaller group also gave us the opportunity for a more personal check-in.

My first small group meeting was led by a woman. When our facilitator asked if anyone in my small group had any questions, I immediately jumped in. I wondered why we were instructed to direct the metta phrases to a *person* when we reached the phase of focusing on a benefactor. My most profound experience of the retreat at the time was feeling my heart break open when I reflected upon how generously Mom Mountain and the whole Earth was my benefactor. This sense of being blessed by dwelling on Earth was heightened by the beauty of the snow-clothed mixed-conifer forest surrounding IMS.

The teacher said it didn't matter who we designated as benefactor but that traditionally it was another human being. I had another question I wanted to ask but decided to hold off, since I'd gone first and wanted to give others in the group a chance. After I'd spoken, one of the men in the group spoke, then another woman began speaking in the slow and careful manner of one coming into voice after eons of silence.

Before the woman could finish speaking, however, she was interrupted by one of the men in the group. This man sat cross-legged in a chair to my immediate right. He not so much sat as perched on the edge of the chair, his body strained toward the teacher. His nose and upper body were leaned so far forward that he looked like he would fall over any moment.

His body was sharply focused toward the teacher; his neck, ears, eyes, and all pointed in her direction. Yes, I looked even though we

SHE WHO HAS LEARNED

were instructed not to. He interrupted the shy woman to tell the teacher how grateful he was for her and her books. He talked quickly about how much harder it was to practice metta than it was to practice vipassana.

"After all, with vipassana you just sit there," he said, "but with metta you direct well-wishes to people, *May you be free,* whether you mean it or not."

He asked the teacher a question, but before she could answer him he cut her off and answered himself. I immediately found his entire demeanor and presentation abhorrent, that is to say, absolutely objectionable; in other words, my mind got on my nerves going on and on about how annoyed I was by his very being. The third time he interrupted someone, another woman, I turned to look directly at him—to hell with the instruction that we weren't supposed to meet each other's gaze—and thought, "Hello, my difficult person."

Immediately after noticing feelings of hatred arising toward my difficult person, I started sending him metta phrases—*May you be happy. May you be healthy. May you live with ease*—with an absolute lack of conviction. My motivations for sending him these phrases were less than pure; they were an act of self-protection, an attempt to prevent the aversion I felt toward him from rooting in my heart.

Another woman began to talk about sobbing in her room the day before, and my difficult person cut in again. He was happy to hear the woman speak about sobbing because she reminded him of another question he had. During our entire session, he seemed to have some comment to make behind or in front of everyone else's. It was difficult for anyone else to get a word in edgewise, as my Momma would say.

I really hated him. *May I be free from danger.*

I hated the situation, and I hated the "nice" silence that we were all operating under. During my previous exposure to vipassana meditation practice, I was instructed to notice the thoughts, emotions, and sensations that arise, in response to what, and what happens to all that arises once we notice what arises in response to what initially arose. Noting or labeling what arises—a thought is labeled "thinking, thinking," for example—helps one cultivate a simultaneously engaged yet detached witnessing relationship with thoughts, emotions, and sensations. I enlisted the technique of noticing to help me deal with my difficult person.

I noticed hating the tacit agreement that we were not to correct one another's behavior but rather merely to take note of our internal responses thereto and to use our observations as opportunities to free ourselves from habitual obstacles to freedom: delusion, fear, aversion, greed, sloth and torpor, boredom. Freedom in the context of our retreat seemed to mean an unflappable sense of interior peace.

Again and again, I noticed the hatred, or aversion, that arose inside of me in response to my difficult person. I noticed abhorring the way the other women did not seem to have room to speak. I noticed being perturbed by the teacher's response, "It's okay," when my difficult person noticed out loud that he was cutting her off and proceeded to do it anyway. I detested my difficult person's habit of talking on and on. I was annoyed when I noted that as he went on I selfishly thought, "God, if he keeps going on, then why didn't I go on and ask all the questions I had in mind rather than being kind and leaving room for others to speak?"

My mind was troubled by my difficult person's behavior, and thoughts whirled round and round about how best to address his outrageousness. Noting the intensity of my strategizing, *"thinking, thinking,"* didn't slow it down one bit.

Drummers' Daughter ascended; her long, thin drumstick-like limbs pounded on my chest. Percussive, her response to Mr. Difficult.

"Stand up to him," she ordered me. "Woman, speak your mind. If his lips get fat, if he pokes them out because he can't stand the way that you stand up, that's his problem. Stand!

"Be as sure of yourself as any grown man. You are free, you have your opinions, you are as bad and as good as you wanna be. I am not saying to do so heartlessly, but, Daughter, you must, *you must* unbridle our tongues. Our tongues cannot be won, one by one. Not until all of our tongues are free shall any of our tongues be free. Be bold. You are a drummer's daughter. Heed me. Be bad. Be percussive. Be rhythmically righteous. Slow your talking down, then quick, fast, change it up. Speak up and down. Be loud. You can bet some other woman will be soft enough for you both. Enough of us have died behind this kind of unequal silence. Break it."

Since I was on retreat and wanted to be good, I ignored Drummer's Daughter's admonishments. I had ample other, more retreat-respectful, options to explore. Should I write a note to the teachers? Should I write a note to my difficult man? We knew each other's names because the teacher had asked us for them during our first interview and they were listed on the bulletin board each day our group was to meet.

I thought of ways to manage my difficult man's behavior at our next group meeting, even if my efforts to manipulate him would transform me into his difficult woman. I thought of ways to speak back to him or to preface my speaking with a verbal muzzle, "Now, if something I say sparks something in you, a memory or a thought or a desire to speak, please wait until I'm done speaking. It is not okay to interrupt me, and it is not okay to interrupt the teacher's response to me."

For two days I practiced various adverse scenarios with my difficult person. I was prepared for him when next our group met. The time came, and this time our teacher was the woman who wrote *the book* on loving-kindness. My difficult person was nowhere to be seen. I was profoundly disappointed. It's hard to put someone in their place if they don't show up.

I did not wait for my difficult man to arrive before I spoke. This time, I began by saying that I had three questions to ask, then I asked them. Given my difficult man's presence in the group, I couldn't afford to be polite. My difficult man came in while I was asking my second question. He did not cut me off, nor did he interrupt the teacher's answer to me. He sat quietly in the corner. I thought, there goes my chance to speak out and make an example for the group of how to address this man's obviously unacceptable behavior, which, incidentally, he was not displaying.

I felt only slightly foolish for once again wasting so much time rehearsing strategies for handling an adversity that failed to arise.

I noticed that my difficult man's behavior did not harm me directly or stifle me in any way. I noticed that I actually benefited from his presence in the group. Because of him, I stopped stifling my questions. A paradox arose: My difficult person was beginning to become an appropriate focus for sending metta to a benefactor.

Once I was done interacting with the teacher, however, Mr. Difficulty came out of his corner and became his objectionable self all over again. He cut the teacher off, he cut off other speakers. He referred everything someone said back to himself. He went on a rant about counting the number of times we say each phrase before, "boom, the benefits kick in, 'cuz we're all aiming toward enlightenment, right? I mean, what is the practical payoff of all this?" he asked.

In one sense, I hated him more than ever, and in another I saw myself in him and hated us both and loved us at the same time. We shared an intensity if not a similar tone of engagement with the practice. I, too, wondered if there were quantifiably cumulative effects of wishing ourselves and each other freedom. I wondered how many times I had to say *May I be free* before actually feeling free from obsessing about my difficult man.

While my questions were not stifled by his behavior, I was still adversely affected. Our group time ran out before one of the women in the group got a chance to speak. The bell signaling lunch rang, the teacher got up and said our time was over, and we all got up to leave. One of the other women, another quiet one, said, "But this sister has not yet spoken." The unspoken woman said, "Oh, it's fine."

What happens to the unsung? Does she die?

But I saw her standing wide-eyed and somewhat shaken at the top of the stairs immediately after the group and attributed the look in her face to not having had a chance to speak in our group. We were not scheduled to meet for another two days.

Anger arose.

A woman's loss of the chance to speak in our group because of what I perceived to be an archetypal, gender-based dynamic was not fine with me. I couldn't bear the thought of suffering through this dynamic for two weeks. Again, the problem rolled around in my heart and mind and came back and back during most of my meditation periods. What to do, what not to do, what to undo and how? Just sitting and walking and noting the experience was clearly not enough.

I noted and respected the impulse that said I had the responsibility and power to skillfully transform a small yet disturbing instance of social injustice. That afternoon I resolved to address the situation in the large-group question-and-answer session. I didn't want to single out or hurt my difficult person. I merely wanted the quality of interactions in our small group to be *happy, healthy,* and to proceed *with ease.* I later learned that my reflections were part of what the Buddha would call right speech—that we were to consider how our speech would affect others before we spoke.

The solution that finally brought peace to my mind was to regard our small group as a sangha, the Buddhist term for a spiritual community organized to nurture each member's liberation. I could then innocently ask about the function of our interview sanghas. I sat in my little room, *thinking, thinking* about my own less-than-enlightened behavior in the interview sangha: making sure I asked my questions first, spending considerable time judging my difficult person's behavior. I wondered how each member of the interview sanghas could honor our individual fears and passionate interest in our own questions while also being considerate of others in our groups, particularly those members who had a slower, more gentle rhythm to their learning.

I practiced different forms of this question in my head several times before the next afternoon question-and-answer session. This happened to be the day that we were to direct metta to our difficult person. When the afternoon time for questions came, Drummer's Daughter thumped on my chest until I found the courage, grace, and opportunity to speak. I asked, "What if the difficult person is not a person but a context?"

Then I gave a brief description of my experience of being personally bugged by my difficult person's behavior but then noticing that it was not merely a personal upset but that it also seemed to go against my idea *(thinking, thinking)* of the purpose of sangha. A community-based frame for my question allowed me to practice metta toward Mr. Difficult and myself and to look deeply at what about his (our) behavior irked me. I confessed seeing a bit of myself in my difficult person. I confessed putting energy into manipulating the situation to serve my own personal needs but finding that my concerns also focused on the quality of the group experience.

But there was much I did not say. I did not say that I was bugged by our collective inability or unwillingness to address the situation.

The expressions on several other sangha members' faces during our interview sessions clearly told me that they, too, were perturbed by my difficult person's behavior. I didn't ask if our vows of silence and self-reflection were vows of irresponsibility to our collective quality of Life. I didn't highlight the odious gender dynamics involved, that a man was monopolizing the talking in the group and that in both cases the teachers he cut off were women.

In some ways I felt like a failure, succumbing to an impulse to change the dynamic in a context set up for us, not so much to change things, as to become aware of them; but I didn't say that. I ended by asking, "What is the purpose of the interview sanghas, and how can they be experienced as extensions of our metta practice?"

The teacher entertaining questions that afternoon was the same teacher who guided my first sangha interview session, a teacher whom my difficult man had cut off. She said that there were many ways to answer my question. She gave us some background into different practices for conducting interviews. She talked about the very formalized practices of one Burmese teacher, Upandita, in which the student first bows to the teacher then talks about what is going well and not so well during meditation practice. She told us that some teachers like to go around and point at everyone and ask what is going on. She said she didn't like that style because she was a shy person, and that style put shy people on the spot.

Then she said, "It would be easy to say that the sangha interview group is part of the world; welcome to it and learn how to deal with whatever is present. On the other hand," she continued, "we are here practicing loving-kindness, so it might be appropriate to ask folks to be mindful of how their behavior affects others, mindful to make sure that all of the people present in the interview get a chance to speak."

While the teacher answered my question, a man sitting in front of me turned around and looked at me. Remember, we're not supposed to look at each other. But I noticed his look; it was not kind, and neither were the stories or names I silently hurled his way in response. I felt defensive under his gaze. I wanted to make it clear that I didn't have the problem of speaking up but that I was having a problem with a group norm that had the consequence of silencing women. I wanted to tell him it wasn't as though I assigned myself the role as protector of women's voices, but my quality of experience in that community was detrimentally affected to the extent that I was a silent witness to what felt like an oppressive dynamic, a historically gender-based one, at that. To silently sit by and witness that dynamic in the name of a spiritual practice was untenable.

When the teacher finished responding to my question, she thanked me for it and said that in speaking up, I probably helped many people. Several women broke the silence afterward to thank me. I accepted their expressions of gratitude as graciously as I could while noting my annoyance at being snatched out of my birthday silence. Other people left thank-you notes and gifts by my door. One of the women who spoke to me mentioned that right before she walked into the meditation hall and heard my question she had come from an individual interview in which she discussed the same kind of troubling dynamic in another group.

We had one more group interview after that, led by the male teacher. The woman who missed her chance to speak in our prior group meeting spoke up assertively and first. Hearing her voice, a note that had been missing, made me happy.

When Mr. Difficult began to cut others off, the teacher cut him off, gently yet surely, several times during our interview. This also made me happy. Everyone spoke, including a woman who sat in with us because an illness had prevented her from meeting earlier with her own group. When the lunch bell sounded, the teacher asked us to stay together until everyone who had a question or comment spoke. He held our ears open, even as one of the quiet women insisted that she didn't need to speak, didn't want to keep the rest of us from eating, no really, it was fine.

While the change to individual interviews was welcome, I missed being part of a group. My interview group was a vocal community of sorts. Like all vocal communities to which I've loaned my tongue, we had our share of missing notes, and hard parts tested the mettle of our voices. During my continuing metta practices, I often thank Mr. Difficult for adding syncopation to our interactions. His voice added an essential element to our collective metta initiation, a kind of hard part that held my attention as rapt as a multilayered rhythmic code that could not be cracked by counting out the individual patterns.

May he live with ease.

DIVINE IS ALSO A VERB

how were you so well hidden
from us for so long?

how are we hidden
from ourselves?

REMEMBER OUR TONGUES can rejoice in the divinity sensed by ordinary consciousness daily.

Divine Daughters. Each time that I've responded with these two words when a woman questions me about my work, I have witnessed a predictable sequence of reactions. If our exchange occurs in person, my inquirer widens her eyes, then cocks her head and stares off into the distance as if lost in or in search of a memory. If we're talking on the phone, first there is a palpable silence. Then my woman friend says, "Hmm." Whether we are face-to-face or ear to phone-assisted ear, there is always more silence.

Then I'll say, "You know,"

the missing
members of our
hallowed families

kin of blessed
mothers, holy
fathers, sacred
sons

When my friend finally finds her voice again, it is often first expressed as cover-up laughter, the kind of laughter many of us release when embarrassed or in pain. Then these comments: "Oh, daughters. Daughters aren't important, are we?" Or, "Good point."

Or, with her arms opened wide, her hands, palms toward the sky, pulsing up and down, the woman before me cries out, "Yes, there is this voice inside of me that I don't know how to let out."

Then more silence. Then ecstatic laughter. Then outrage. Or resentment. Or shock.

One friend, a psychologist, breaking the usual mode of response, said, "Every mother who has a daughter knows daughters are divine."

Yet when I asked her to speak to me of her knowledge as a daughter's mother, she balked. There was silence. She who is usually articulate was not. She said daughters' divinity is too much like breathing, too automatic—I said like heartbeats, like gravity receiving our feet—to describe.

Digging deeply into the cross-referencing pages of Webster's *New World Dictionary* for the origins of the word *divine,* I find: "of God, inspired by God, sacred, holy." I find words that my mind was socialized to attach to the faces of white men. I remember stained-glass pictures that I was raised to believe depicted a supreme, white male being, and pictures of a luminous Mary and male child, pictures wordlessly making clear the blessedness, the holiness surrounding those who bear and nurture sons of the divine.

Digging even more deeply into Webster's, I find *divine* rooted in these words: gleaming, shining, evoke, to call on for support. These words remind me of what is perpetually expected of daughters of every age: To gleam. To be the pride-inspiring apples of our fathers' and our mothers' eyes. To be luminously supportive. Always available to be called on as helpmate, playmate, woman in the omnipresent, powerful Others' wings.

Gleaming, shining. These words also evoke memories of Life's unbiased generosity toward daughters.

Remember or imagine consciously resting in the unseen yet real vibrancy in which we draw each breath. Remember or imagine dancing in the company of other daughters drumming and dancing in the dawn. Remember or imagine being stunned by a soft sun shining through a beaded sky, a sun sparkling through rain. Remember or imagine being held in the one-eyed gaze of a low, full moon's almost vocal gleaming. Remember or imagine the young daughter of a friend crawling into your arms to give you much-needed hugs. Remember the grace that sometimes comes in the quiet, after being searched for, struggled for, grace that comes as a surprise in the quiet of exhausted pausing.

Remember to relish natural glory. Remember to gather with other awakening, luminously juicy daughters. Again and again, remember to echo interior wisdom into welcoming ears.

THE DAUGHTERS OF ZELOPHEHAD

once we have heard
just once
deeply heard your names
interior elder sisters
just once heard all daughters
hold all the people
there will ever be
inside
before ever breathing a breath
being pinked out
learning to be tasty
and everything nice

divine daughters
life will for us be different

S OON AFTER FIRST SINGING "Glory be to our Mother and
Daughter," I began to ask all my priest and preacher friends
for stories about divine daughters.

Being my Momma's daughter, I started my search for the missing
members of the hallowed family by questioning authorities in the
Christian church. Momma's Lawd is often all up in my mouth, especially in times of need or perplexity, as in the prayers "Lawd help"
or "Lawd, have mercy" or simply "Lawd, Lawd, Lawd." Momma's
Lawd and church are supreme authorities in my extended family.

My sense or lack of self and confidence was immeasurably influenced by a Momma with the Lawd in her mouth.

Momma robins feed their babies worms. Mine put her Lawd in my mouth, along with his mandate that only daughters who were supremely self-sacrificing were good. Seemed to me that while Jesus lived to serve, he also developed his numinous capacities, and that such development was integral to Christian definitions of goodness. I found it odd that in my years of attending both Sunday school and the grown-ups' church services every Sunday, singing in the senior choir from the age of ten, and knowing almost all the parts to most of the songs in the hymnal, that I'd never heard one song or story of daughters' divinity and how to develop the same.

As a child, I couldn't imagine getting away with truly emulating Jesus. Once, when I questioned an elder's spiritual understanding, as I was told Jesus did, Momma's powerful backhand helped me fly over the dining room table without benefit of wings. The first two times Momma sent me flying, I got up and continued questioning her friend, Miss Neal. The third time, Momma apparently knocked all memory of what I questioned out of my mind, and her kind of sense in. Unfortunately, she also knocked in the notion that questioning her or any older Black person about spiritual matters was a dangerous proposition. Only in adulthood did she tell me that the way I questioned and not the questioning was the problem. Meanwhile, I spent years wandering around in a spiritual wilderness, uneldered. There was no one close to home with whom I dared discuss my deepest aspirations, wonderings, and fears.

Somebody needed to have mercy. After witnessing the powerful effect Voicestra's singing "Glory be to our Mother and Daughter" had on audiences wherever we went, I began to search for the missing members of the hallowed family. Surely, other daughters had walked paths parallel to mine, through cultures even less hospitable to daughters' unsanctioned shining. I was determined to find divine daughters' stories, to learn and sing my spiritual elder sisters' names.

Imagine living in a culture saturated through and through with Life-affirming stories and songs of daughters whose freedom— singing through millennia—could help others echo our myriad ways home. Imagine a group of daughters, a group to which you and other daughters whom you love belong. Remember that all women, no matter how old or how young, are daughters of the voluptuous earth. Imagine this group being as small as two best friends or as large as a generation. Our task is to bring into being the institutions, ideas, and creations required by our evolving species. Like bats, we echolocate nourishment and danger by sending out our voices and listening to the shapes of the echoes that return. By call and re- sponse, we make our ways through the mysteries of what each of us must discover we are best suited and called to create. We send out voicings—sonic probes—of barely audible yet essential questions and insights encountered as we work. We send out calls for help. Our voicings often happen at frequencies barely audible by the ear yet known by heart, like a beloved chant sung over and over. Our successes or failures reflect our collective ability to hear and respond to one another's calls.

My lifework with thousands of daughters of many ages from around the globe leads me to believe that by nurturing the audible light of daughters, our species will draw that much closer to realiz- ing our creative promise. I reason that the profound absence of an- cestral divine daughters' voices is an augury that we are equally un- prepared to create resonant ecologies—vibrantly sympathetic environments—in which to cultivate contemporary daughters' bril- liance. Our abilities to nourish daughters' visible and audible luminosity are deeply influenced by our abilities to recognize the same. Repetition, or the lack thereof, deeply influences recognition.

Imagine a world bereft of our beloved vocal wonders: opera, gospel, indigenous people's voice blessings, and our favorite children's songs. Imagine life devoid of Negro-Colored-Black- or African-American spirituals. Imagine a world as empty as that! Without the many resonant chambers of the body, especially those created by the holes we have in our heads—nostrils, mouth, sinuses—vocal wonders, as we have known them, would never have lived. Voice requires resonance.

Divine is a verb as well as a noun. To divine—discern, discover, intuit—daughters' shining often requires restorative and protective measures. All too often, daughters' authentic voices are lost in adolescence when the cacophony of parental expectations, peer cultures, and mainstream media emphasizes image over substance and selfless devotion to others. In my personal experience and work, without a counterbalancing, articulated, and culturally embraced reverence for daughters' perceptions, girls learn to subdue their essential selves, to discount their encounters with the divine. Subjugated girls tend to become subjugated women—many of whom become mothers who pass on their ways of turning down the volume of their lives in the name of survival.

Resonance doesn't discriminate between Life-affirming and Life-denying effects.

What Life-restoring creations are extinguished or delayed when we cut divine daughters' voices out of memory, off our tongues, and risk losing our ability to divine daughters' creative voices? I discovered that such risk is ubiquitous throughout Judeo-Christianity. In religions dominated by men, women usually accrue merit only as wives or wives-to-be, as mothers or mothers-to-be. Daughters' divinity is subordinated even in religions dominated by women, according to scholar Susan Starr Sered's book, *Priestess, Mother, Sacred Sister*. The most salient mythic and symbolic roles in female-dominated religions are enjoyed by mothers, grandmothers, and sisters.

The ordinary reality that millions of daughters throughout the earth are denied reflections of our indwelling sacredness, just as we are, both sickened and spurred me on in my search for divine daughters' voices. I was disheartened by the initial responses to my inquiries. Questions about the identities and fates of divine daughters generally drew kindly, empty stares from priests, preachers, deaconesses, church Mommas, and countless masters and doctors of divinity.

A Black Baptist minister and dear friend who told me he envisioned God as a dark chocolate woman was the first certified holy person to give me enlivening information about divine daughters. He told me about the daughters of Zelophehad, five sisters whose voices transformed rabbinical law.

We know their names: Mahlah, Noah, Hoglah, Milcah, and Tirzah. We even know what some of their names probably meant. Milcah, for instance, is a feminine form of the root *mlk*, which means ruler or leader. Milcah has been interpreted as an honorific description of an individual's familial position. Be patient; you will soon know the importance of this etymological detail.

Mahlah's, Noah's, Hoglah's, Milcah's, and Tirzah's father died before reaching the promised land. He died in the desert. He died without male heirs. Tradition had it that because Zelophehad was sonless, his name would be lost from the roster of Israel, and his portion, his place in the promised land, would be lost by his next of kin, his daughters.

Mahlah, Noah, Hoglah, Milcah, and Tirzah were Zelophehad's daughters, of his house, his offspring, recognized by his kindred as being of their tribe. But as daughters, they had no precedent to rest upon in claiming rights to any land that would have been their father's had he lived.

The land was the basis of living. The land was where you grew food, where you belonged. The land rooted you in tribal reality. The land was promised to those who remained faithful to YHWH. The land was reward for heeding the words of the prophet, Moses, and leaving the house of bondage. The land was the ground of freedom. The promised land promised to make all the wandering and suffering worthwhile.

The promised land, the refuge, the locus of being, was close at hand when Zelophehad died.

It was probably Milcah, the leader, who called her newly fatherless sisters into a meeting. The Bible is silent about this part. But my imagination is loud.

"Sisters, we must speak to Moses before the tribal priest and the chieftains," Milcah said. "We must ask for the promised place in our father's name. His name is our name, and we must not let it be erased from Israel's roster. We must submit a plea that it is unjust to exclude daughters from inheritance rights. We must ask the prophet to appeal to YHWH for what is justly ours."

Looks of dread crossed the faces of two of her sisters. The other two laughed. One of them said, "It is taboo for a woman to make such an appeal in front of the tribunal."

"We'll stand at the doorway," Milcah said.

"At best, the elders will laugh us away. At worst we'll be stoned," another sister protested. "Milcah, the heat and our years of wandering in the desert have affected you. Come here, dear sister. Lay your head down in my lap and rest."

"At best, YHWH will say yes, Zelophehad's daughters are right. At worst we'll be doomed to a homelessness that is the same as death,"

Milcah said. "With no name in the books and no place in the promised land, we're at the mercy of our kin's generosity or avarice. What do we have to lose?"

The sisters looked deeply into one another's faces. They knew Milcah spoke the truth. With neither father nor dowry, they would be forced to accept whatever men asked an uncle for their hands in marriage. Why should they die with their father's death? Why lose the shield of his naming, a branding they had borne since breathing their first breath? What was the harm of risking ridicule if that which stood to be gained was a liberating leverage: land?

"Please, just agree to go with me, and I'll speak for us all," Milcah said. She wasn't named Leader for nothing.

Putting dread aside, they lined up, with Milcah no doubt slightly in front, to state their plea to Moses, Eleazar the priest, the chieftains, and the entire assembly. The biblical account would have us believe they spoke in unison and said:

> Our father died in the desert
> and he was not among the gathering that gathered themselves
> against YHWH, in the gathering of Korah.
> But he died for his own sin
> and he had no sons.
> Why should the name of our father be removed
> from among his family
> because he has no son?
> Give unto us a possession among our father's brothers!
> (NUM. 27.3–4).

From "The Will of the Daughters," by Ankie Sterring, in *A Feminist Companion to Exodus to Deuteronomy,* ed. Athalya Brenner

So wise, their speaking, clearly implying that their actions arose only out of their daughterly concern that their deceased father's cherished name live. Wisely they spoke: three times they established their father's faithfulness, established that he was no rebel and, by implication, that neither were they, despite their unprecedented, bodacious questioning of YHWH's will that the land be divided among the men only.

The Bible says Mahlah, Noah, Hoglah, Milcah, and Tirzah blended their five voices into one. An interpretation: their tongues became the tongues of all daughters questioning the messengers of Gods whose laws were unjustly silent regarding daughters. By asking that such an oversight be corrected, Mahlah, Noah, Hoglah, Milcah, and Tirzah spoke for us all.

In response, YHWH told Moses:

Rightly the daughters of Zelophehad do speak.
Give, you shall give to them a hereditary possession among their father's brothers. (NUM. 27.7).

By divine decree, not only did the estate of Mahlah, Noah, Hoglah, Milcah, and Tirzah (we must remember *their* names) become hereditary, but also their case became precedent.

The saga continued.

In Numbers 36, we learn that the chieftains of Zelophehad's daughters' family were distressed by YHWH's divine decree. What if Mahlah, Noah, Hoglah, Milcah, and Tirzah married outside of their tribe? According to custom, husbands usually came to own their wives' possessions and, eventually, became their heirs. If Zelophehad's daughters married outside of their tribe, their land would be passed to the tribes of their husbands and thereby would disrupt the balance of land-based power in Israel. Of course, such imbalances would never do.

The chieftains brought their anxieties to Moses. Moses decreed, in YHWH's name, that heiresses to real estate must marry paternal kin.

Which the daughters apparently did by marrying cousins. Yet, they still had to ask, again, for the land of their father. This time, they based their request on Moses' words.

We do not know if Mahlah, Noah, Hoglah, Milcah, and Tirzah lived happily ever after. In my Momma's way of seeing things, they made the best of what they had. This is a quiz: Of the following possible interpretations, in which voice will you pass on the story of Mahlah, Noah, Hoglah, Milcah, Tirzah, and their father Zelophehad: the voice that says that despite the sisters Zelophehad's outspokenness they were still subordinated women, or the voice that says, given their context, they spoke with wise tongues?

The story of Mahlah, Noah, Hoglah, Milcah, and Tirzah whet my tongue for more stories of daughters who elucidated divinity as they lived an out-loud devotion to freedom. I sought a diversity of named and unnamed, individual and collective, daughters' liberation strategies sung from many lands and tongues, singing a rich legacy of divine, daughterly behavior.

I sought and found more legends, historical accounts, folktales, tribal creation stories, and contemporary customs recognizing daughterly divinity than can be detailed in this one volume.

A Filipino woman told me about an ancient mountain-based priestess school and secret society that survived colonialism and continues to exist on the island of Lison. I found Apache ceremonies for asserting and cultivating daughters' divinity from birth. I found "Daughters of the Puna" Incan women who, in order to follow the wisdom of their Mommalines, settled on plateaus or "tablelands" of the Andes Mountains rather than submit to Spanish rule. I found voice maps of women's wisdom leaping the mountains between India and Tibet in many tongues. I found Mahapajapati's successful campaign for the ordination of Buddhist women. I found Harriet Tubman bodaciously stealing her parents into freedom.

When courage flags, I remember these daughters. When cultural conditioning catches my tongue, I remember these daughters and sing out as best I can, even if alone. I dream of amplifying divine daughters' heart-giving (encouraging) voices of possibility and inspiration to as many daughters as ecological integrity will allow.

My commitment to ecological integrity requires me to ask what it means that the pages of *Divine Daughters* may have once been alive and upright, as trees in an ancient forest. While I've questioned my publisher about paper sources and have received assurances that this book probably doesn't contain ancient trees, the chances that it does are still very real. This is a tree-clause book, which means that we plant two trees for every one used to print the book. The publisher matches the money I donate for this purpose. Is this restorative effort enough?

What were my alternatives? Broadcast the names and lives of divine daughters via radio? From where does the power source for broadcast media come? Depend on word of mouth to spread the good news of daughters' divinity? Are you willing to help? Are you willing to read *Divine Daughters* aloud in groups of friends? Are you willing to recite sections of *Divine Daughters* by heart in the middle of a crowded elevator as you rush to work?

My assignment: to divine the voices of daughters who lived lives that belie cultural categories and dichotomies. I sought daughters who gave tongue to both spiritual and political wisdom as they sounded a way out of no way. I found daughters who were individually distinct and collectively effective. Their shining living evidenced a Life-restoring discernment of our true and untrue differences based on race, color, class, and gender.

Books dedicated to the stories of women who "make a difference" are all too often silent about women's spiritual lives. In activist circles, I am often implicitly asked to check my spiritual life at the door. In spiritual circles, I am often encouraged to transcend political concerns. Imagine asking Harriet Tubman, who prayed and sang her way out of slavery, to separate her spirituality from her politics. Imagine asking the Daughters of Zelophehad where their politics began and their spirits ended.

In *Women Who Run with the Wolves,* Clarissa Pinkola Estés amplifies the old tales of wild women, many of which had been altered into anemic versions by the time they reached our ears. In *Women in Praise of the Sacred,* Jane Hirshfield amplifies the women's voices in "the wide chorus of the world's sacred singing." Collectively, Estés and Hirshfield write about outcast daughters, celebrated poets, educators, political leaders, queens, courtesans, leaders of religious communities, exiles, scholars, spiritual adepts, housewives, intellectuals, members of prayer circles who sang prayers called "ring shouts," recluses, Nobel Prize winners, Christian and Buddhist nuns, priestesses, saints, healers, women who owned vast wealth, and women who were owned: daughters all. The tongues preserved by Estés and Hirshfield hint at an ancient, Earthwide echo of daughters' vocal wisdom. These singers are one another's spiritkin, they are our elder sisters, they are Life's daughters, and they are—in my book—divine.

We call "divine" certain experiences or perceptions that are nourishing, mysterious, and unconfined by cultural boundaries. We call "divine" that which can be neither wholly contained nor created by our species. Divine daughters' tongues are like that: whole. Their voices echo out through the ages to offer other daughters a quality of nourishment that we may justifiably honor with the name divine.

Please do.

DIVINE DAUGHTER SISTERS: LOVE YOUR CELLS

If I were with you I would whisper this in each of your ears:

Love your cells.

This is the most powerful secret I know for developing the discernment we need to divine daughters' divinity. Love your cells with such a deep, deep love that they'll tell you beyond questioning, beyond doubt, if an action or belief or emotion you are considering will do you harm or good.

This secret is kept secret by those social forces that exist to sell us artificial salvation in lieu of the nourishment our cell-based discernment would guide us to receive freely from Life Itself. I would whisper this truth to you not because you must keep it concealed; on the contrary, whisper it to as many beings as you deem open to hearing it. I would whisper this soul-saving secret to you because you must hear it with both your inner and outer ears.

That I would speak this at all respects your outer ears. That I would whisper respects your inner ears' enormous sensitivity and fluency in the soft-spoken languages of dreams. The whisper is a most intimate way of exchanging information. The information exchanged in whispers is not limited to the sounds or meanings of words. If I were with you I would whisper this secret, *love your cells,* about which I speak to you instead magically through the silence of this page. I would whisper it close enough to your ears for you to feel the warmth of my breath, the heated gift of our green elders, the plants and the trees, who constantly give us the very air we breathe.

Test this with your nearby daughter sisters; do it as a favor to me. The next time some image of who you should be confounds your sense of a freer, essential being, ask one of your beloved daughter sisters to whisper into both of your ears, at least nine times:

Love Your Cells.
Love Your Cells.
Love Your Cells.
Love Your Cells.
Love Your Cells.
Love Your Cells.
Love Your Cells.
Love Your Cells.
Love Your Cells.

Move gent - ly _____ in - to your ___ a - ris - ing __ Go sure - ly ___

a - ris - ing We are sis - tahs ___ Go - ing __

_ with - in un - know - ing Grow Move gent - ly _____ in - to your

Know - ing __ We are sis - tahs ___ a - ris - ing

_ a - ris - ing Go sure

We are sis - tahs ___ Go - ing

What are the seasons of the sung?

What are the sung's bringings up and comings 'round—higher, higher—to another rung? What are the sung's reasons for our coming into being and to voice?

How does the sung's tongues grow from seeds of sound found first in the ear? In the womb? In the bone? Where, the sung's bodily home? How do Life's sounds take root in our beings, freely singing?

Excerpt from "Sistahs," written by
Rachel Bagby. Copyright 1993
Breathing Music ASCAP.
Used by permission.

FARMER'S DAUGHTER

II.

I am a farmer's daughter

daughter
of daughter
of daughter
of women
who
knew
what to plant
during which growing moon

I am a grandchild
of harpist

music of growing things

OLD TIMERS 'ROUND HERE in New Hampshire call this Mother's Day snowfall "farmers' gold." Farther south, in Philly, Momma rests up on her Sunday. The moon is still what she calls wasting, what others call waning, its luminous face getting smaller and smaller each day. When its glow starts to grow again, Momma will plant her seed sweet potatoes.

Another name for farmers' gold is "sugar snow," I tell Momma over the phone. On this day, her day, I bet' not miss calling my Momma. Talking with her, I riff on her South Carolina sweet tongue, moving back and forth between southern and New England dialects. We love each other out loud. Long-distance, we nourish each other with stories of what we've done when and what we plan to plant soon. We nourish each other with stories and musings. Our talk is music of growing things.

We're making beds now, but we won't be planting them with those p'tatoes during this wasting moon, Momma says. But least we're done foolin' with the snow. *Good* gracious, girl, how you stand all that cold?

How you stand all that noise, Momma? I ask, as the doorbell in Momma's house rings for the umpteenth time and, even long-distance, I hear a chorus of children's voices chime out: "Happy Mother's Day, Miz Bagby."

When Momma returns from receiving her gifts and cards and giving all of the children candy, she tells me that most of the group that just left won a prize last year for their garden. Envy arises. Momma was too busy making do—being the cleaning lady at my elementary school by day, attending Temple University for her teaching credential at night—to teach me to garden when I was young. Momma tells me the forty or so vegetable and flower gardens she has helped the neighborhood plant are getting to be too much for her in her elder years. She hopes some of her older students will take over soon. She says the trouble of noise interrupting us ain't nothing, compared to how she used to be troubled over the purse-snatching boys who used to hide in what are now gardens but used to be empty lots.

Thank the Maker, Momma admonishes. I'm grateful we can do all we do. Close to a hundred houses we've fixed up that would otherwise be filled with crack and broken babies. Girl, don't mess with me 'bout noise.

Yes, ma'am, I say. Even though it's snowing, it's not so cold, I say, eager to get back to our conversation, eager to head Momma off from preaching a long-distance Mother's Day sermon. She umm, umm, ummms when I tell her the growing season here lasts a mere ninety days. But, Momma, I say, all year long we're living in poetry. That keeps me warm.

I tell Mom a sweetness comes of the barely here warmth's intercourse with the not-yet-gone cold. Where warmer air meets air cold enough to make snow, maple trees go into orgasms. Then the trees' sweet sap flows like that of a satisfied woman, I tell my Momma. The maple's sap is tapped, then cooked into syrup.

Like you like on your pancakes, Momma, I say.

Momma says, girl, stop talking your foolishness. Her tee, hee, hee tells me otherwise, tells me, go on. Obeying Momma's laughter, I tell her the wisdom behind calling spring snow farmers' gold.

A January warm spell melts all the snow that was here in early winter. Sixty- and seventy-degree temperatures for weeks give us an early mud season. The old timers 'round here call this season "January thaw." And bulbs and the green of the grasses, dandelion, plantain, and heart-shaped violet leaves are hoodwinked by the warmth into peeking out of the ground.

The snow that falls after January thaw is wealth for the farmers because it turns pre-spring new greens back, back into the earth. The dirt receives the energy. The sprouting leafiness is immediately composted under an undulating vibrancy of cold-warm-cold-warm-cold dirt.

This falling white stuff is also called "poor man's fertilizer": a gift from the earth to poor men and women living dirt-to-mouth, growing food for their families. How generous, how voluptuously rhythmic this otherwise reserved region becomes as winter tussles with spring. Yet many who are neither farmers nor their offspring— Earth's daughters estranged from the land—protest snow-borne poems and sing out for more sun.

daughter
of daughter
of daughter
of women
who
knew

To deeply be of a place and a people means knowing their seasons and languages, speaking their tongues, singing their music of growing things, knowing and loving their names.

My Momma's Momma was Grandmom Eva, a mixed blood: Scottish and India Indian. She played the Celtic harp in her Scottish father's Baptist church for colored people. Grandmom Eva's father was called colored even though he was Scottish with white, white skin, Momma says. (What's in a name?) He was called colored because he married colored, and therefore with colored he belonged. His daughter played the Celtic harp of his people amongst colored people and sang Christian songs.

Grandmom Eva's Momma's name was Elizabeth Minerva Simianne Texas Jennings. Great-Grandmom Liz. Matrilineally, she carried my *daughter of* stories and songs across multiple bodies of water to plant in America. She came to South Carolina with Great-Granddad Jennings's family. She came unfree.

Before Great-Grandmom Liz, our *daughter of* stories were sung by women whose names we may never know. I only found out about Great-Grandmom Liz upon returning home to my Momma's house, at the age of twenty-five, in search of what I was missing: *daughter of* stories and songs. I was sent home by Mom Mountain to find the sources of what sang me so wild and vulnerable walking her. She said that listening to my Mommaline's singing was required to keep me alive. A voice as clear as the sun talked to me as I walked

Mom Mountain. A voice clearer than the water running down Mom Mountain's sides knew better when I said I was never going to ever set foot in a city again.

It must have been Mom Mountain who told me I had to return to my Momma's house or die. Every inch of any me I knew *knew* better than to seek freedom there. At the age of seventeen I could barely wait to get out, out, away from Momma's insistence that I appear acceptable—in thought, word, apparel, and pressed hair—to people she had to live and work with. At seventeen, I thought that developing the powers of voice that were my birthright as Life's daughter required rejecting the voices of my female human ancestry, the *daughter of* stories that danced as my blood. I thought I *could* reject those stories, reject the very need to know my Great-Grandmomma's Elizabeth Minerva Simianne Texas Jennings name. I thought whatever stories had shaped Momma would sure 'nough strangle me, since Momma tried to shape me with a suffocating hand.

Mom Mountain's must have been the voice that deemed my freedom dependent on retrieving *daughter / of daughter / of daughter / of women who knew* stories. No internal voice that I recognized as mine would dare point me toward Momma's house in search of freedom.

I did not want to be daughter. Ever since learning that being a daughter seemed to be the cause of so much that hemmed me in, I did not want to be a daughter.

Daughters grew up to be women, and I did not want to be a woman. Being a woman looked like caving in. It looked like a shame-filled snaking around. It felt like being in slavery to men and a white god. It felt like a prison. It felt like an eternal metal clothespin clamping my Life-given powers and voices down, a closing opened to give others pleasure and offspring, then clamping down again. It felt like no breathing room, no ecstasy, like being a daughter meant having a mouth that said yes to the world's requests, yes to what promised to bring pseudo-acceptance, and no to the heart's requests to be loaned a voice for sonorous insights and dreams.

I watched Momma silently deal with this double-tongued madness. She became the cleaning lady at Pratt Arnold, my elementary school, when they wouldn't hire her as a teacher because her credential from South Carolina was considered inferior in the oh-so-superior Pennsylvania school system. The school officials who called her training inferior based their decisions on prejudice rather than on an assessment of my Momma's knowledge and skills. Yet their prejudice, despite its inherent untruthfulness, was the basis for their refusal to hire her.

That they would not hire her is a fact. That she then became a cleaning woman to be close to my brother and me and to influence our education positively is also a fact, and is heroine-ic.

The teachers at Pratt Arnold Elementary School were Momma's prayer partners and neighbors. They were women and men who attended our church. They were a sister-in-law and cousins, people with whom she marched on city hall to protest the elected officials' habit of denying services to our neighborhood. Momma also marched into my classrooms to jack up my teachers in front of all my peers if she strongly disagreed with what or how we were being taught.

Some of the teachers looked down on Momma, and I sometimes felt ashamed, because she was a cleaning woman. Other teachers did not, because they knew and admired her undercover strategies.

As the cleaning woman, she was often privy to what the principals planned before the rest of the school knew. Paper shredders weren't in such widespread use in the late 1950s in Philly. I did not know at the time how much Momma's embarrassing trash-picking habits enriched my life. She was used to having legitimate access to administrators' ears. Her questions about the need for cleaning supplies would segue into her questions about, say, getting her fast girl chile into the accelerated program at Mastermann Middle School.

Momma got seriously interested in dirt that only she could see when certain folks were talking as she cleaned the main office. She seemed able to make herself invisible, staying real close to the ground, closer than she already was at barely five feet tall. In the late fifties and sixties, a golden age of assimilation, Momma listened hard for opportunities to integrate me into the best schools Philadelphia could offer.

With hindsight, I admire Momma's audacity and wisdom and ability to shape-shift so easily from underling-obedience to Momma-ferocity. Even at the time, I loved having access to every teacher's room—all that colored chalk!—and each and every book in the library before and after hours.

But I also saw Momma take lip from teachers who were younger than she, younger and mean to cleaning ladies. I watched her sweet-talk and yessir and yesma'am administrators, and I got slapped for sassing some of them back. When I asked her why she took what she did in silence, she quietly told me, "Just so, just so." She told me that since we were women, such was our lot. She showed me how to snake around it.

How could I be such a woman? Don't make me be such a woman. I cannot be such a woman. I have to run away as fast as I can from being a woman. I can't stop running until I am no longer any kind of woman at all—whatever it takes. I can't stand what happens to women. I can't stand what happens to men, but at least as a man I can yell someone outta my face, I can run faster and farther and put something up—my dukes, a gun—and make others shut up.

I can't keep writing this. My arms fly up on their own, and my fingers flutter in air, in memory of flight, and this is flight, and my feet are shuffly, shuffling uncontrollably beneath me as if I'm running, and my breathing is as fast as one running, running, running, running forever to escape the skin I'm running in, and I can't be a woman, I can't. I won't. Being a woman is too lonely, too hard, too heavy, too thankless, too nowhere, too empty, too godblamed set up.

I pretend I'm a son. Their powers seem most powerful. I refuse to grow breasts larger than the buds that popped up before I thought I could choose not to be a woman. I keep my hips small. I cannot, will not be a woman at all. Fingering the air, straining to be outta here, I refuse to be woman.

Writing is edged by sobbing. Deep, deep this anguish of the broken woman line. Childlike the sobbing, the heart-level gasping for air, shallow the breathing, hurting the forehead, snotting the nose. Slow, the typing through this pain that now moves to my belly. Ugly, my face feels ugly, these lips spread ugly, curled under and wide like they sometimes are when I'm singing.

Watch real singers, really singing. Live. Sit close. Watch what they do with their mouths, instruments that don't always look pretty. Stop watching. Don't demand pretty. Be moved by sound.

I went to Mom Mountain to try to hide from being a woman. She sent me home. She sent me back to my Rachel Edna Samiella Rebecca Jones Bagby Momma for the stories of the women in my family.

They made a way outta no way all of their lives. Not all was pretty. Not all was lived out loud. Great-Grandmom Liz came here with nary one other member of her kin, leaving behind who knows what family and where. She knew, days before, when big storms and rains were coming by the whispers they sent through the air. She lived through Civil War–torn South Carolina and lived to be 104. When it was time to leave this Earth, she fed her chickens, swept her kitchen floor, sat down, and died. She knew the prophetic powers of dreams that somehow passed on to me despite my Momma's moving up North, despite the near-fatal neglect of our *daughter of* stories and songs—neglected in Momma's struggles to make ends meet on our narrow, brownstone and brick-house-lined, North Philly street.

The prices we paid for progress, for getting as close as we could to acceptance by white folks (read *acceptance* as so-called decent lives, good money, a house and lawn of our own) included fried hair, schooling that often severed the elders from young ones, neglected *daughter of* stories, rejected divine daughterhood, many cut tongues.

Better to cut our own tongues than to be hung from a tree by a Klan who thought nothing of taking a torch to what they called uppity niggers. (What's in a name?) So my Momma's people did not talk about the past because her family lived on a forbidden edge of intermingled skin. And then someone burned Momma's father's house down because he had too much. And her womenkin were raised to be quietly effective. From all sides, my Momma learned not to talk.

My life required talk. When Mom Mountain sent me home, I was crazy for lack of the women's stories. I had become an educated fool, rich in high-priced degrees, alienated from the dirt-rich vocal wisdom of women who, as Momma says, "have lived some," women who knew when and how both to hold their tongues and to grow back previously cut ones.

When I told Momma my life depended on her telling me the stories of the women in our families, stories to protect and guide me in what often felt like a no-women's land, she instantly dropped a lifelong taboo. She remembered, she regrew, her *daughter / of daughter / of daughter* tongue.

She remembered and spoke of training to be a midwife with my Great-Great-Great-Aunt Lula. She remembered a remedy for women's troubles: bark from the long-leaf pine's sunrise side. She remembered digging red root and wild onions and helping Aunt Lula hang everything up to dry, just so. She told me her apprenticeship, which she began at age four, ended abruptly because she couldn't stand the sight of blood.

Momma spoke of the sound of Great-Grandmom Liz praying in her room behind closed doors. What you heard was the whirl of her heavy skirt hitting the floor, Momma said. What you saw when she opened the door and stepped out was a face fulla something that looked like she swallowed the flame of a candle the family later relit and used for evening prayer.

Momma remembered spending her childhood summers with Great-Grandmom Liz, cleaning out chickens, getting chased by geese, making butter by shaking cream up in a jar really fast and singing to it: *Come, butter, come. Come, butter, come.* Momma remembered spending her summers with her Grandmom, learning how to read with her eyes and her nose and her ears, lips, skin, and tongue what was being brought up, what was coming 'round, and how to prepare for it all.

Listening to Momma, I hear Great-Grandmomma Liz giving me, the daughter of her daughter's daughter, ancestral assignments. From three generations ago, from a seemingly infinite number of growing and wasting moons, from Cope, South Carolina, Great-Grandmom Liz sings:

thishere is where we started in thishere country
where and how
this road we called the dividin road
kept our family together
kept us safe

from a war misnamed civil
from the South's ropes and fires
from kinfolk slaughtering kin over colored
paper and shades of brown skin
under cannons and greed and control
over lies and ripe fields

hundreds of acres in front of dividin road
belonged to Jennings, a Scot
your great
great grandfather
his side saw to it
not one *tich o'* trouble troubled us

the hundred behind the dividin road
Jennings gave me and my husband
his eldest boy Jen

him
I nursed as a baby
ayah I was called in India
unsacred cow

being fifteen years Jen's elder
his paid-for Momma
my skin dividin-road brown
made us two
no never mind
though seems like the census had fits
over what to call our seven children

white one year
colored the next
mulattos after
call 'em whatchu want census man
betchu they all got through college
have mercy
betchu they all got their piece of our land

my middle daughter was your Grandmom Eva
her first chile who we called Simi
married Billy B.
A Black man from Phillydelphia
they had your brother then you

remember this chile
remember where and how we started
know whatchu carryin on
all those roads you say own you

find your folks Freedom, Someplace
Rachel Bagby
find us a peace filled place, chile

WHAT TO PLANT DURING WHICH
GROWING MOON

IT SEEMED THAT NONE of my accomplishments—graduating from Stanford Law School, passing the California bar on my first try, helping to establish an institutional home for the Martin Luther King, Jr., Papers Project—helped me fulfill my ancestral assignment of finding a peace-filled place called home for my Mommaline. I took my ancestral assignments seriously. From the time I first learned about three-greats-Aunt Lula and Great-Grandmom Liz, I began opening my life to their resonant wisdom. This was difficult to do in the cracks left from serving on several committees, coordinating Stanford's African and African American Studies (AAAS) program, writing and producing my first play, answering the undergraduate students' calls for a knowledgeable professor of African American literature rather than the white graduate student studying with Sandra Drake—daughter of the renowned AAAS scholar, St. Claire Drake—before her illness threatened to cancel the class. Then, I was busy, busy, busy securing funding for the King Papers Project's building, furniture, and staff; busy anchoring foundation stones for stories of the United States' Black freedom struggle as told by prominent men.

In the process, I came across stories of the women who started the Montgomery bus boycott. Women, members of the Women's Political Council (WPC), most of them teachers at the local college, gathered data for years about incidents of brutality suffered by women and children and men on the public buses. There were the stories of young girls refusing to give up their seats to white men and being dragged off the bus for their audacious, symbolic speech.

There were tallies of the increase in domestic violence correlating with waves of brutality suffered by men at the hands of white bus drivers.

Black folks had to pay in the front, get off, and reenter the bus through the back door. It was not uncommon for the driver to pull away before the Black rider could get back on. The atrocities suffered were tallied by the women of the WPC, and they agitated for a boycott for years.

They even had the mechanism in place for responding to the right moment, whenever it would arise. Flyers would be mimeographed and distributed by students. Blacks would forsake the buses to walk, share rides, do whatever was necessary to break the economic back of a public transit system that required their patronage to run.

The freedom of Black people was served by women who wanted to be free of the insult and danger, inconvenience and inequity suffered daily on the public transportation system they used to go to work. Some folks made money by operating jitneys that served as alternatives to public transit.

During the boycott, many "day" employees—maids, cooks, childcare workers—lost their jobs because their employers sympathized with the bus company. Many white women, out of loyalty or dependence upon the women who ran their households in a manner to which they had become accustomed, became their helpers' chauffeurs.

I felt more turmoil, not peace, as I learned about the stories of the women and the men who were active in the Black freedom struggle. I created multimedia exhibits in Stanford's student union so that whosoever wanted to could learn what our forebears suffered so that we might live and breathe and sing and speak more freely.

I became obsessed by the question of how those before me could do what they did and not hate. How did they stand being hosed down like cattle, witnessing their daughters blown apart in church, enduring their sons missing then found, murdered and bloated in southern rivers, and not hate? How could it be true that the spirituals they sang and the voice of Martin Luther King, Jr., breathing life into the Bible's stories would be strong enough to help them do all they did and not hate? What nourished their courage? How did their faces become the very faces of peace while subjected to so much hatred?

I took my ancestral assignment to find a peace-filled place seriously. Yet the heavy hand clothed in racism's velvet white glove, more finely dressed yet no less arrogantly ignorant in Stanford's halls of privilege, seemed to signal that the apparent peace of freedom fighters from the sixties was foolish or at best untrustworthy.

But they were my ancestors and many of them, still alive, my elders. I knew whatever freedoms I enjoyed were partially paid for by their blood, and my own was on the line for coming generations. Still, I longed for a freedom that felt more free than that which required me to hold my tongue constantly in deference to professors, mostly men, whom I was informed were the lords of the land. I needed a freedom that didn't make me feel like piecework: the mouth and mind welcome in the name of advancing the careers and histories of men, the body's need for rest, nourishing food, and tender caressing habitually ignored.

No Shakti, no peace.

In the languages of India, my Great-Grandmother Liz's homeland, there was at least a word, *Shakti,* that recognized daughters' spiritually rooted and physically evident creative power. Not only was this power named, *Shakti,* but the generosity of air required by its proper pronunciation, the play of its consonants—where the *k* meets the *t*—bespeaks the polyrhythmic whispering of vivifying essence.

Shakti. Shakti. To say the holy name of *Shakti*, again and again, call-and-response in a circle of daughtersisters/sistahfriends is to become a communal rattle, a *shekere,* a living, chanting *ache* (ah-shay): the communal expression of spiritual power. The word *Shakti* contains the power it names.

No Shakti, no peace. My life was devoted to the legacies of those who fought and died for justice. This was my calling. In another place and time I would have been trained as a praisesinger. I lived to keep alive the memories of those to whom we owed our freedom. I lived to help those younger than me remember and live true to our legacy. My working for justice was a given, given the skin I was in, my Mommaline and my Daddyline, and my own inclinations.

But there were few trustworthy people in my world who knew of my need for wise counsel and nourishing acknowledgment of Shakti.

Luisah Teish, an artist, activist, and Yoruba priestess whom I met at a women's gathering on spirituality and politics, intuited this need in me and suggested I attend a retreat entitled "Black and Female: I Know the Reality." Correction: Teish *insisted* that I go. She said the retreat was offered by the Bay Area Black Women's Health Project, and even the name felt good to me. Teish said the retreat was a place where women who worked hard to help other women could go and rest and get clearer and stronger together. Teish said "Black and Female: I Know the Reality" was a place where I could experience healing and the foundations of peace: an inner awareness and release of whatever it was that clamped down on my Shakti, my numinous, daughterly power, and rendered each accomplishment necessary yet insufficient to fulfill my ancestral assignments.

I often sensed a brown, naked, famished being within that looked somewhat like me sitting on my heart. But my heart looked like a little

WHAT TO PLANT

stone, and the sun-baked turd of a being sitting on it acted as though its hardness was her throne. Her emaciated long brown finger raggled at me, as did her jaundiced eyes, as she constantly spewed out my inadequacies. This I-had done wrong, and this and this. That would some day be the end of me, and that and that.

Teish said, "Black and Female: I Know the Reality," and I heard *refuge from my tormentor.* I heard resting place. I heard sisters there gathered who could listen to my life and hear what I said, hear with understanding because they'd been where I'd been, known what I'd known, and knew to come together to heal what only got reinjured again and again in the world.

Teish said, "Black and Female: I Know the Reality," and I heard sonorous mirrors that acted like canyons, echoing back what was said in a healing chorus of uh-huh, we are sisters, and I know that's right. I heard the possibility of calling out and receiving a healing response.

I went.

The workshop, led by Lily Allen, was sponsored across the country by the National Black Women's Health Project. The format was simple and ancient. We gathered. We told one another the stories we dared not tell anyone else, not even ourselves, not completely.

We were encouraged to tell the group our deepest, forbidden reality. We were invited to release what we felt the most shame about, a shame that sapped our regenerative powers. We were told that we were safe to tell one another the truth and that doing so would help all present reclaim our birthright of vibrant health.

Lily claimed that what we refused to tell at least one sister was killing us as much as any other stress we faced: ordinary racism, systematic denial of the truth of our womanhood in the stock images of Black women saturating the press. We knew that we weren't stereotypes. We were full women, not only Mammies, Sapphires, Wannabes, Welfare Queens, Church Mommas, Cleaning Ladies, Affirmative Action Upstarts, Apologists, or Adversaries. We knew the deeper realities of why our mothers didn't know how to teach us to truly love ourselves. Self-love was so often seen as a luxury for a people still working on mere survival. We knew that the habits of silence our ancestors maintained in the name of surviving slavery's brutality with dignity had appropriate and inappropriate expressions in our lives.

I knew that I 'bout died before hearing the stories of the women in my family. I knew that the seductions of assimilation almost rendered me deaf to the sustaining knowledge that Great-Great-Great-Aunt Lula knew about bloodroot and bark from the long-leaf pine's sunrise side. Momma told me she didn't think Great-Grandma Liz's and three-greats-Aunt Lula's stories were important to our survival in the North, even though Great-Grandma could tell a storm coming for days, and storms respected no region. Even though what Aunt Lula knew about the sunrise side of the long-leaf pine helped heal many a woman, and the white doctors often turned to her for help with their hopeless cases. Mom had her hands full of keeping us fed and clothed and sheltered and helping us get into "good" schools that would groom us to slip into the doors cracked open by affirmative action. No one around me had the thought in their minds to make sure that I also tended to that which no amount of money or privilege or white folks' approval could buy: *Shakti!*

Momma said she didn't think those stories were important. Surely, they couldn't be as important as learning how to get me in the best schools the city had to offer, and not as important as working two jobs to earn money for me to attend to college. The women's stories could not possibly be as important as learning how to navigate the public records at city hall to learn who owned what empty lots and dilapidated houses so they could be snapped up and turned into award-winning gardens, fixed up and sold to the neighbors at cost.

The women's stories, surely, could help neither Momma nor me learn how to stop shy of too-tired-to-eat before we stopped working for others. Those stories, most probably, didn't have practical remedies for what happened to us regularly when the demands of city-life got on our very last nerve. Learning what we needed to learn and finding the money we needed to find to help Miss Lady's children down the street or to pay for the bar review course so that I would be sure to pass—all this was more important than taking time to talk about all the too much trouble we'd seen, and taking time to release that trouble from our cells.

Wasn't no use crying over spilt milk—what Black Momma's daughter didn't know that? We were raised that to be strong was to be silent and to ignore the signal of bad feeling, to not let the bad feeling show. At least, in a world so hurtful to us, where even home was no haven so much of the time, we would not let on just how hurt we were. We'd be strong and tell ourselves that whatever happened, we could adapt, and that would be that. To let someone else see our tears, to sob out loud, was to wallow in feelings that were just 'soon better not felt. What good did feeling them do?

Lily and the sisters supporting her told us that we could collectively hold any sister's pain, any sister's anger, any sister's shame, any sister's story told or sung or trembled or screamed or punched out in the name of healing. She told us that giving these sources of our self- and cell-denials to one another's ears would heal both the hearers and the heard. She said that in witnessing one another, in listening and receiving and giving love to the depths of our beings, we would work miracles. "Black and Female, I Know the Reality" promised us the freedom of reclaiming powers locked away in our forbidden, forsaken interior lives.

We were called out of our hush harbors and into a realm of public healing. We were called into full feeling. We were told that we were finally safe to tell and thereby unbelieve the unspoken and unspeakable fates that the dictates and dictators of racism said were our due. We were invited to know that we were worthy of fully, freely being. We were invited to tell what we had suffered and how we had triumphed. We were invited to know and speak and see and hear that there was room enough in our shared experience to have been snatched and burned by stories of deserved damnation and to reclaim ourselves as whole again.

We were invited to sing ourselves holy, to accept redemption in our sisters' faces, in our own voices and names. We were offered the possibility of learning that we could and, indeed, must sing ourselves home again. We were told that by so doing we would help all the other sisters who shared our stories to also come back home. We were reminded of our legacies of shared healing. We were called to heal in the cadence and color of our ancestors called to tribal rituals that in their Christian incarnation had become the moaning bench.

We felt the blessed continuity of being called to communal healing. In the name of Life, we would be transformed. And our acceptance of the call would be sealed with baptism, for the waters of the Pacific Ocean sprayed upon the very buildings where we gathered. We were at a national seashore facility, a former barracks reclaimed from the military and now used to host workshops and naturalists' programs. Yemaya, crashing outside our retreat windows, lent her *ache* chorus to the call.

Something deep within me responded. I felt a freedom singing in me that seemed to pull me up out of my chair. If not there, where, I wondered, could I confess to having loved one white man, having been raped by another, and having allowed yet another to destroy any remaining shreds of dignity during a month of homelessness and daily marijuana smoking on El Camino Real in northern California?

Only with hindsight did I label that period of my life as evidence of self-hatred, a natural outcome of the devotion to a kind of assimilation in which white culture is held supreme. At the retreat, I listened to myself tell the stories of my white period in an emotionless monotone. These were the facts: I'd wanted to be white, to receive what looked like the goodies bestowed on white people. I believed the propaganda I saw on television, only in hindsight could I say foolishly. The suburbs looked so peaceful. Living in such peace, which I so longed for, was possible only if I were attached to a right white man—not *the* right white man, mind you, but the rightness of whiteness and men.

So what if it meant living in dingy motel rooms, with a screaming cat on my lap, a cat unschooled in self-hatred and emotional suppression. She howled out a discomfort I wouldn't allow myself to feel. Two nights in the Motel 6, three in the Cozy 8, and then back to the Motel 6 for a week. The white man with whom I lived this way was twenty years my elder. The way we lived was his idea of freedom. We ate out. We ate up my meager savings. Looking back, I knew I was crazy.

But at the time I was caught on a wheel of delusion that didn't seem to stop. And the home I remembered in Momma's house didn't appeal to me in the least. Was my father's behavior more hateful than my own? What possessed me to embrace a life of such degradation?

The marijuana I smoked daily seemed to drain me of all ability to act on my own behalf. When I finally got free enough to get to a so-called intentional community I was raped on the first night by one of the residents as he called me goddess.

Divulging this, I cried. I didn't have to say another word. The women heard and listened. Teish, sitting in the front row, cried with me. Another sister, unnamed, unknown, unseen but heard in the back of the room, started a low, lulling hum. I stopped talking, started sobbing.

We were encouraged to feel what we had buried deeply within us. We were encouraged to release, to talk, to express, to tell stories and feel feelings, to be heard and loved beyond all that we had suffered and in spite of and because of it, anyway.

We were planting freedom in one another's ears. With our listening and our voices, we prepared a new ground for our freedom, a knowing that we were not alone. We breathed with the understanding that all of our doings were not of our own choosing. They were some blend of conditioning and desire, degrees of skillfulness and desperation. We had acted on half-information and outright lies, false images and beliefs. We gave voice to our acts in a context of blessedness that gave every woman gathered in the room the womb of our sisterhood in which to heal.

Such a feeling I could not explain—to know that I was received by at least several sisters whose eyes said, we love you, as we love ourselves, *regardless.*

I looked and I saw that I was their neighbor, and their love meant something, because we knew something that everything our ancestors and we had gone through could not snuff out. We were there in the name of our collective beauty and power and healing, and our being together was very, very good.

After each divulgence, I looked into the eyes of the sisters looking at me and saw acceptance, compassion, and even some looks that said, "been there." As I careened out the pain of reliving the multiple betrayals of self and other, sisters lifted my moans up with their own, and we sang ourselves into release. For the first time in memory,

WHAT TO PLANT

I was in a vocal and healing community that accepted me as I was, accepted our moments together as opportunities for healing. The Lawd didn't even think of leaping into my mouth in the presence of those sisters singing me home, though I heard the Lawd's name in the room and was comforted to have it there.

Sisters talked and prayed together, hummed ourselves and one another on into the waters and over to the other side of crying. Our tears released sorrows our Mommalines had carried for generations. We watered freedom for ourselves and one another; for our elders and our youngers, daughters all. Our chorus of humming, sweeter than honey, evoked that of sated baby bears.

Stop crying. Shut up. Eat your food. How many daughters have swallowed these bitter words? What kind of nourishment can a woman receive with a belly full of uncried tears? The fields of our creativity were flooded with forbidden sorrows or filled with the rocks of unforgiven pains or aflame with the fires and fists of stifled anger. We don't even have names for the indigestion and malnourishments of Black women, the eating disorders we typically face of being too busy listening to another sister or feeding a brother to eat. Too many of our guts were too twisted denying our feelings in obedience of a mother's admonishments to deeply receive the nourishment of food.

But at the retreat, we fed one another our ears. Our tongues were an easy emetic treatment. Up, out of our guts, all sorts of sorrows and angers flared. The humming sisters hummed us all into staying present while Lily worked with woman after woman to the point of release. The hugging sistahs hugged. The rubbing sistahs rubbed. The tissue-bringing sistahs gave one another tissues without the stifling of emotion that can come from such ministrations. Somehow, we meant it when we agreed that we were there to be honest and present with our feelings.

When I sang, there was room enough for me. When I sang, there was no rush of time, no insistence that I make anybody happy or feel like the price they paid for the admission ticket was worth it. I sang freely, like I was only used to singing in the presence of trees or while walking Mom Mountain or standing on a bridge, listening to the music made by rock-troubled waters.

When I was done, I had confessed my desire to be white when it became clear that some white woman would win the John Robert Powers Finishing School Modeling contest, even though the most beautiful contestants were us colored girls, if you asked me. I confessed deciding that I would marry a white boy to have access to their kind of power in the world if my classmates at Stanford Law School were right in their perceptions that no matter how good I got I would never be one of them. Somehow I thought I could be one of them if I learned what they learned and thought like they thought. I thought that succeeding at becoming a white boy would really be the best that I could be. I confessed every last heinous detail of self-hatred I now knew to call by that name. And, after each disclosure, when I would emerge from my cloudy vision, emerge from the gong in my ears as I traveled back and forth through time, emerge to look out at the sistahs looking at me, I saw no malice. I heard, welcome home, girl, welcome home. I heard, chile, you been gone away from home too long. I heard women in the background humming for me like I often hummed for others.

I let out a whoop and a holler. I sang from the bottom of my lungs, and my guts emptied open and strong. I sang out my gratitude and harmonies. And the women present joined me. Though this was the first time I'd laid eyes or voice on all but two women in the room, they all wrapped their healing tongues around the sound dripping out of me like they knew this music since we all were born.

Something in our bones knew, *knew* the sounds of freedom waiting to rise up out of our throats, knew the blessings our voices could and should and would be to and for one another. And we blessed one another freely. And the hush that came when we were done let us know that we had never really been alone and always were alone in the home where the sung hung out before belonging to anyone.

And the moon was growing and growing.

With the heaviness lifted off my heart, I sang and sang and sang. One woman would talk story as we walked, and I'd sing my response. In the dining room, with other sisters in singing, I lifted up this or that song. Spiritual, chant, praisesong, lullaby, singing in tongues—music had its way with me that weekend, and it was good, very good. Felicia Ward, codirector of the Bay Area Black Women's Health Project, said, "You need to sing with Bobby McFerrin. Have you heard him?"

I'd gotten used to that response whenever I sang out of an inner freedom.

It is fall 1982. I am working as a law intern for one of the founders of the Bay Area Lawyers for the Arts. My assignment is to organize the recording contracts of Windham Hill Music. I sing as I work, as I so often do when working alone, filling the air with first this part, then another of the multilayered music only I can hear in its entirety.

At the end of a task, I take a breather, go drink water. Ned, my supervising attorney, asks, "Have you ever heard Bobby McFerrin?" I haven't. Ned suggests I give him a listen, go to one of his concerts and see and hear what he does.

Early 1983. I'm in Music Annex, a recording studio in Menlo Park, California. Two friends, a woman on violin and a man on piano, are helping me record "Listen." It is the first of my original songs and spiritual assignments I've subjected to the world of engineers and sound boards, mikes and mike shields, multiple takes,

editing, reverb, isolation booths, and no windows for the sake of
sound integrity.

Waiting for the engineer to complete his preparations, I softly
sing a rhythmic melodic line, oh, so softly. Autumn, the violin
player, hears me and asks, "Have you heard of Bobby McFerrin?
You need to hear him sing."

Ned and Autumn and Felicia and all the others who said I should
hear Bobby sing were right. Listening to Bobby's spirit singing
opened up a new season of singing in my life. It was not only all
right but fun to sing aloud what Life sang inside. Not only was it
fun, but if I got good at it I could earn part of my livelihood singing
what I now sang for free everywhere and anytime Life so moved me.

I first saw Bobby as Bobby alone, at the American Music Hall in
San Francisco. My then-new boyfriend, Martin, and I hooked up
with Jake, one of Martin's college buddies, and arrived early enough
to get seats right up front. We also met Beth Arnold in line, someone
Jake knew from their shared place of worship, Saint Gregory's
Church. We laughed together, talked. Beth joined us, and we had a
mouth-side seat in front of Bobby. We sat so close I could see how
his nostrils slightly flared sometimes when he took a deep breath.

Joy. During his concert, Bobby noticed Jake and Beth—he knew
them from St. Gregory's, said hello, asked me my name. I laughed
my response: *Rachel.* Bobby made fun of me, mimicking each hiccup
of a sound that laughter interjected in Ra-hee-ch-ha-ha-l as I simultaneously complied with his request for my name while gasping with
glee that he'd noticed me and invited me into his performance.

Whether cutting the fool, as Momma would say, or singing a
prayer of gratitude to Jesus, Bobby displayed a mastery that the
music playing inside of me insisted I needed to cultivate. Before
hearing and seeing Bobby, I had no idea how to meet the demands
of the inner singing. After meeting Bobby, I devoted myself to it.

My next experience with Bobby happened in the context of an early version of Voicestra performing in the round at Noe Valley Ministry, a church and performance space. Several of the Voicestra singers I would later sing with sang that night.

The singers entered and fanned out into a circle with Bobby at the center. Some placed bottles of water at a safe distance behind them. Their entering set the air alive with a cross between electricity and the quality of air around waterfalls. Their very presence was both enlivening and refreshing.

All you could hear was breathing. We, the audience, were seated in chairs encircling the circle the singers made around Bobby. As he began giving out parts, lines from a chant came to mind: *we are in a circle / within a circle / with no beginning and with no ending.*

Once the singing began it did not end. Bobby would add a part or change a part; signal to someone to solo, solo himself. One song transformed into the next and another. I was transported by the round-and-round, shyly and quietly joining in with the melodic line whenever so moved. Toward the evening's end, Bobby walked around the outer circle and, miraculously, made the word *God* feel okay in my mouth for the first time in years.

We were singing some praise of God's name, and Bobby gave the audience parts. I sang a harmony to the melodic line Bobby gave my section of the outer circle while clapping one rhythm on my left thigh, drumming yet another on my right, and tapping out a polyrhythm with my feet.

If omnipresence and omnipotence were grander than what I felt, participating in an infinity of harmonies and rhythms, then God was all right with me. If the singing we now set ringing in the Noe Valley Ministry was just a taste of the glory we all happened to call God, then God was all right with me. If God was a noun we used for the verb be-hind the best we could hope to express with our joined voices, if pictures and images and sounds and names were simply portals through which we entered the luminous realms of Life Itself, then, I tell you, ecstatically and sonorously, the word *God* was all right with me.

Then and there, my dream of singing in Voicestra took root.

I wanted to study with Bobby. I needed to study with Bobby, but he wasn't taking on new students. He was too busy raising a family and touring and nurturing the recording career that would earn him five Grammys in one year.

True to being a farmer's daughter, I planted more than one seed of my dream of living in the freedom of Voicestra's heartfelt singing. I studied breathing with Rhiannon, formerly of Alive! and the award-winning a capella group SoVoSo. I went to a Redwood Records workshop on creating a singing career by someone who knew of what she spoke: Linda Tillery. Linda, founder of the Cultural Heritage Choir, alto and percussionist extraordinaire, has recorded and performed with too many stars to name, for fear of insulting someone by leaving them out. A skilled record producer and gospel music diva, Linda became a legend in her time when she threw down a malfunctioning mike and could still be heard as she belted out a sizzling R & B number at the open-air Greek Theatre in Berkeley, California.

I did not know then that years later I'd be sitting in a circle with both Rhiannon and Linda and that along with the other daughters in Voicestra, we would come to call ourselves the Stra Fems, collaborating on other projects as sistah singers. I simply followed where led by my voice and the Life planted in me by Daddy's drumming and Momma's music of growing things.

When Felicia Ward and other sistah singers at the "Black and Female: I Know the Reality" retreat asked me about Bobby, I said, yes, yes, I've heard him and Voicestra sing, and I dream of singing with them; pray for this dream to come true.

After the retreat, Felicia and I gathered with other sisters to sing. I drove down from my tree house in the redwood forest of La Honda to meet them in Oakland. Other times they braved the snaking, one-lane road up to my place. And we sang and sang.

Over the next two years, I made several trips to Oakland to sing with Felicia and to help with fund-raising for the health project. On one fateful trip, she greeted me at her door with news about a master class Bobby was teaching at Omega Institute in Rhinebeck, New York. Participation in the master class was billed as a step in the process of auditioning for Voicestra.

Felicia remembered my prayers and kept her eyes open for me, have mercy. We were daughters actively devoted to each other's dreams. I had asked for prayers in support of my aspiration of singing with Voicestra, and Felicia opened her door with an answer in hand. I sang, and the nourishment I sought for what Life bid me sing was found.

Bobby was admitting only twenty singers in his class. To audition, we had to submit a cassette of no more than ten minutes. Several of the selections had to be original. And I had only a week to create, record, and submit my material. I needed to overdub several voices to send Bobby a halfway true rendition of the several pieces telling me they needed to be in his ears. I didn't have access to an inexpensive multitrack studio or the sense to ask around to see who could help me find one.

Being the daughter of a make-do queen, I asked myself what Momma would do if she were in her equivalent of my situation. She would use whatever she had on hand for the job, or she would call a neighbor.

At the time, my tree house in the redwood forest abutted Portola Valley State Park. I couldn't see my nearest neighbor and didn't know anyone around for miles. For all I knew, someone else in the forest had a recording studio, but I couldn't imagine little colored me knocking on my neighbors' doors: *Excuse me, I live in the tree house up the way. My name is Rachel Bagby. How are you today? Please, I know it may seem odd to have a lone Black girl walk up and ring your doorbell in the woods, but please don't slam the door in my face. I'm just wondering if you happen to have a home studio and would like to work with me for a couple of hours. I've got three days to record ten minutes of original music so that I can study with a vocal master I've idolized for years. His name is Bobby McFerrin. You may have heard of him. President Bush loves his song "Don't Worry, Be Happy."*

No, I lived outside of the neighbor solution without which Momma never would have been able to keep our family alive. I did, however, have two answering machines and a boom box on hand.

I recorded the melody on one answering machine, then recorded me harmonizing with the recorded melody, then played the recording of the melody and first harmony on the boom box while singing and recording another harmony line. The sound quality was rough, but the ideas were clearly communicated. I hoped my song titles were evocative: "Of the Divine," "Don't Wait," "Ms. Do."

I got in! Then my only challenge was to budget the money for plane fare, ground travel, four hundred dollars tuition for the week, plus room and board. The whole affair would cost a bit over a thousand dollars, which seemed like a fortune at the time. It seemed a crime that I'd have to journey all the way from California to New York to work with Bobby, when he lived only forty-five minutes up the street, so to speak.

But a thousand dollars was a small price to pay for what promised to be vocal heaven. Remembering that my brother, Nelson, had gone to music camp for a month in the Pocono Mountains of Philadelphia every year, from elementary through high school, I was happy to finance my own musical dream. Here I was thirty-two years old and just now getting around to seeing what that slice of the privileged one's life was possibly like.

At least that was the plan before the IRS attached my bank account and emptied it of my savings to apply to a delinquent tax bill of a few thousand dollars. Life, have mercy. I told Beth about the tragedy, and she immediately said, give a concert and raise the money.

What would I do on a stage, alone, for over forty minutes? I asked. What did Bobby do? Sing. Clown with the audience. Pray out loud. I liked the idea. Beth suggested talking to the dean of Stanford's Memorial Chapel to sponsor the affair. He was an Episcopal priest, and Beth was studying to be one. I arranged for the three of us to meet for lunch at the faculty club to discuss the possibility of sponsoring a music series, a musical ministry, at Stanford and calling it, "Who Sings at Memorial Church?"

The idea was a natural. The dean professed loving music, especially jazz, especially Bobby McFerrin. Tuck Andress and Patti Cathcart lived in the neighborhood, and with Windham Hill headquarters right down the street, we'd have no lack of talent to participate in the series. My concert would be the first and a benefit to help me raise the money I needed to go study with Bobby. I'd also sell copies of the audition tapes. The community that loved and supported my work would be sure to come out for my send-off.

They came. The local paper ran an article announcing the concert. A friend, Aleta, danced beautifully to "Grandmothers' Song," music I'd recorded for the soundtrack of *Alice Walker: Visions of the Spirit*, a documentary by Elena Featherston. I improvised while strumming an old space heater that had a harmonically tuned face guard of metal strings. I improvised with four people I brought up to encircle me, telling the other observing audience members to be patient, creativity takes time.

The concert was a creative and financial success. The moon was so new that the mystery of its being was invisible in the night sky. So, too, was the time awaiting me at Omega Institute.

WHAT TO PLANT

SING WHAT YOU HEAR

*S*O THIS IS THE BIG WOW, I thought, my heart's POOMpoom
POOMpoom a timpani accompanying the squeaky van wheels
along the backroads of Rhinebeck, New York. I was on an
aptly polyrhythmic journey to a five-day master class with Bobby
McFerrin.

I was one of the chosen few, one of twenty vocal artists Bobby se-
lected after hearing audition tapes submitted by one hundred eighty
hopefuls. He said he prayed to pick people who would be good for
one another. Our focus for the week: dynamic singing.

Bobby gathered us together for the purposes of practicing ways of
releasing the possibilities within each note and learning how to click
into improvisation. When I called the end-state he wanted us to
achieve "being outta the box," Bobby laughed in agreement.

He started our shared adventures in sound by saying, "Let's get
the scariest thing out of the way first." Meandering his foot across
the hardwood floor of a dance studio we were about to transform
into a sound box, he said, "Step into this stream of music and sing
what you hear."

When I stepped into music's stream I 'bout drowned. Five melodic
lines jockeyed to be the first one out of my mouth. I changed choruses midstream each time I ran out of breath. My heart's POOM-
poom POOMpoom was audible as a subtle tremolo on my sustained
notes. Bobby's eyes, the only lifeline I had, registered each melodic
leap. I kept hoping that a thread capable of holding the myriad
melodic lines together would reveal itself. It didn't. Crazy quilts may
be beautiful, especially if there is something that connects each piece
to the other, some shared chromatic theme, some same color of

shiny silk thread, some explosion of color so loud, so brash as to be the blindingly obvious focal point. But my five-minute improv lacked an audible center and was too effervescent, too fragmented to be satisfying.

Bobby was kind. He reminded each of us that we were there to learn. "Relax," he told me. "Grab one musical idea, hang onto it, and take musical breaths." *Click*.

Something inside of me *clicked* into alignment in response to his words. I knew this thing about musical breaths was an essential element of Bobby's musicality, his apparent ability to sing three or four harmonies simultaneously by singing just enough of each one, jumping back and forth between them, to create an illusion of sonic continuity. Bobby gave our ears enough of each harmonic line to hear a pattern and fill in what we should be hearing while he sang yet another line. His in-breaths advanced the rhythmic element of what he sang and sometimes even carried a hint of tone.

Something deep within me, deeper than my ability to act on that understanding, understood that breath could function as connective tissue rather than as the mechanism for jumping from one melodic idea to the next. With breath as connective tissue, an improv could be circumambulated until its essential center was sung, embellished, sung again.

Click!

"How you breathe is as much a part of your composition as the sounds you make," Bobby said. Such a simple revelation, a cornerstone in Bobby's musicality, became the path beyond what was previously possible with my own voice.

Paying attention to the breaths in an improv gave me another method of listening. The rests became as important, if not more so, than the doing of singing. In the rests, the whole pattern could be heard a bit louder than seemed possible while singing, singing. Even though multiple ideas continued to assail me whenever I lent my mouth to music's stream, breath helped me choose the few that could be sonorously woven together into a whole, satisfying song.

During my week at Omega, many, many songs were born with all their parts—pleasingly integrated rhythmic, melodic, and harmonic lines born of the moment, born in response to the moment's needs. Attention to my breaths deepened my experience of singing as a form of prayer.

From practicing musical breaths, a secret to Bobby's ability to create seamless walls of sound, to learning about the musicality he picked up as a child crouched under his father's piano while Robert McFerrin, Sr., taught others how to sing, we found our week filled with insights about the spirit of listening, performing, and teaching. Breath by breath, Bobby's prayers that we all be good for one another were answered.

On the first day of the master class, one of us admitted feeling like a puppy dog ready to lick Bobby's feet, thus articulating the embarrassing performance anxiety attending our hero worship of Bobby. Even though the wider public knew him as the voice that brought us "Don't Worry, Be Happy," a song that became wildly popular when appropriated by George Bush's presidential campaign, we knew him as a singer's singer.

We oohed and ahhed his ability to consistently produce crystalline tones. We marveled at his control over a four-octave range, a rarity among singers. His skill at improvisation and innovative arrangements of classical, jazz, and popular music had earned him multiple Grammy Awards.

Bobby generously took us through vocal paces to open the inspired center in our own voices and aspirations. He also continually admonished us to stay connected to our spiritual guidance to sidestep the formidable hot spots of the music industry. When one classmate lamented that if you haven't "made it" by twenty-one, you might as well stick to typing, Bobby said, "I didn't even begin to take myself seriously as a singer until I was twenty-nine."

Hearing Bobby's story, I began to feel that it was okay that I was thirty-two before giving my first solo concert. Still, I felt inadequate to the music that claimed me as its own. What I heard within my inner ear had no chance of living outside, if my mouth alone was to be its instrument. I needed a transcriber, someone who could easily transcribe symphonies and choral glories as intricate as the *Messiah*. Inside, I heard voice upon glory-filled voice, singing and being sung with Life's praises. This is what I heard when Bobby sang.

He seemed to move so freely into the quality of breathing that creation, mystery, solitary musical revelation, and shared ecstasy had in common. He seemed to be singing me so often when he opened his mouth. That he affected so many people the same way told me he sang with an integrity to which I aspired. If anyone could teach me how to be true to the music singing in what seemed to be the core of my being, Bobby could.

After hearing him the first time, I had attended every known concert he participated in within a ninety-minute drive. When he'd appeared at the New Varsity Theater in Palo Alto with the dynamic jazz duo of guitarist Tuck Andress and honeyed-alto Patti Cathcart, I sat near the front. When the audience joined in, Patti and Bobby heard my voice and turned my way. I had studied with Patti briefly, singing an original song on our first meeting when she asked to hear something from me. She'd said, "From what you sing, I can tell you aren't afraid of giving your voice to spirit. Now we'll just work on the instrument."

Attending the week-long master class with Bobby at Omega Institute was an unprecedented chance to work on my instrument. But while being in the presence of Bobby encouraged me to be true to cultivating the vocal spirits claiming me as their own, it also opened me to being assailed by my demons of inadequacy. NOstopDON'Tcan't-NOT visited me regularly at Omega. On the first night, before we met as a class, I saw Bobby in the café. He was sitting one booth away with Debbie, his wife. I wanted to go up to him to say hello but didn't. I was the only other Black person in the room. I wondered if he recognized me from the concerts in the Bay Area. Unlikely. He was a celebrity with many faces seeking his attention. People were crawling all over him. Bobby, Bobby, Bobby. I decided not to add my clamoring voice to the others. I was sure he needed rest.

Part consideration, part fear kept me from his table that night and kept me tangled up all week. He said he would offer us individual coaching, would talk about our aspirations, would offer suggestions for what to focus on as we improved our technique. He promised to discuss our possibilities for being one of the eight voices he sought for the version of Voicestra he planned to work with for a year.

We were the privileged few. It was "art week" at Omega, and several people told me they'd hoped to get into Bobby's class. When they didn't, they enrolled in their second choice, planned to take Bobby's sampler, and constantly asked those of us in the class to teach them what we were learning.

One woman told me she wanted to apply but couldn't afford studio time to make her audition tape plus the $425 tuition (almost double what the other courses cost) plus airfare from Montana. As I listened, I thought better than to tell her how I got there and the gifts of preventing NOstopDON'Tcan'tNOT from getting in my way.

Another woman, Victoria, who has since become a dear friend, entered the bookstore and started making the most outrageous sounds, getting us all singing. She told me she was second on the waiting list—how lucky I was to get in!—and that she had studied with Bobby at Omega the year before. The center of me was content to accompany

Victoria's vocal gyrations with polyrhythms tapped out on a flat ceramic frame drum. The edges of me felt intimidated by Victoria's passionate freedom in singing with strangers. Her energy fired the bookstore up into brilliant song. If she was second on the waiting list, what powerhouse singers had made it into the course?

Fears and feelings of inadequacy arose and fell. Fantasies of performing with Bobby that week visited in waking and sleeping dreams.

How to describe vocal heaven? Bobby envisioned taking a year off to create an ensemble of eight to sing for soundtracks, to travel as a group, and to have fun. I immediately began to scheme free time from my full-time job as associate director of the Martin Luther King, Jr., Papers Project at Stanford. Documenting the Black freedom struggle's history was important. But not everybody heard the music I heard, nor were their ears singing with Life's music.

I had found this out when everybody and their Momma started walking around with a Walkman tape recorder and earphones glued to their ears. I had feared for folks and the damage that constantly listening to the radio and other people's music would do to the music of their souls. Only then had I discovered that not everybody heard Life the way I did. If what Bobby sang was any indication, we were kindred musical spirits. Life willing, with Bobby's tutelage, I would learn how to create a life true to my song-filled soul.

As fantasies go, this one was as true to life as they came. I saw from the reactions folks had to the twenty of us who got in what could be in store for me if I successfully realized my aspiration. People's faces went into subtle and not-so-subtle frenzies whenever we said we were in Bobby's workshop. "It's a privilege," my improvising friend in the bookstore informed me, "a tremendous privilege and blessing."

I was the only Black person in Bobby's master class. I wondered how that happened. Yes, the price tag was steep and I'd never heard of Omega. But it was in New York, and surely folks in New York knew about it. Bobby's hit, "Don't Worry, Be Happy," wasn't nationally known when the master class was first advertised, but it had zoomed up the charts before the class was held. I spent a little time speculating why no other Black folks were present. There I was again, *the one*. Thirty-two years old and still not used to it.

Wow.

My journal notes from the week are splattered with succinct suggestions for developing vocal and performance technique.

Breathe musically. Begin concerts with 15–20 minute warm-ups: singing. Do tongue exercises: Bideda Didela. Breathe musical breaths. Choose one idea in the stream of music and stick with it.

When Bobby accused us of not knowing what to do with our tongues, I begged his pardon. The group laughed. The bawdy humor I honed in my childhood neighborhood often gets me branded as a hussy, but at Omega I barely cared. I was in heaven and having fun. I could only imagine what it was like for my brother, Nelson, to have had a month of focusing on music, in the clean air and trees of the Pocono Mountains, every year for eleven years. I wondered where my music would be if I had been given that opportunity or had even known to ask for it. The hour upon hour upon day upon day of singing was a heaven for me.

I felt so pushy when it came to making my individual date with Bobby. It seemed so difficult to find a time for the two of us to meet that I began to feel that Bobby was avoiding me. He must have recognized me as the same woman from the Bay Area who wanted to study with him. Maybe my sense of humor made him want to stay away from me. Or maybe he felt how desperately I wanted him to teach me, teach me.

But I was no more eager than any of the other Bobby-rabid people in the class, no more demanding, no more desirous of his attentions. One woman said she felt that when we opened our mouths we were actually at such risk of judgment that we were in danger. I didn't feel that, though I was mindful lest I make too big a fool of myself. I was there to learn as much as I could. Another woman in the class, Janet, seemed so relaxed when she sang. She said singing was like playing. I decided to emulate Janet.

The work, joy, and pain of being a professional musician were never as clear to me as they were while I studied with Bobby. He was highly successful, in terms of popularity and having a hit song. He was also road weary and wanting to give more time to his family. Our tuition was so high, in part, because he needed to bring his wife and two children with him to Omega. We also paid for the privilege of being in such a small class. Had Bobby been willing to work with more people, our experience would have been less intimate but more affordable. Ah, the economics of ecstasy.

On our day off, the day Bobby was picked up by a limo to go to Leonard Bernstein's birthday party, I danced with Baba Olatunji and source rhythms of Nigeria. Baba told us that we needed to get together and save the world. He said we should take our energy of joy out with us and spread the consciousness and healing in our communities at home. Baba sounded like my Daddy and Momma reconciled: *Dancing and divine generosity. Drumming and the free movement of our bodies part of the good and healing time. Creating because we are creation and that very fact brings all around us joy.*

The next day our intensive work and my journal notes on singing à la Bobby continued.

Practice singing the interval of tenths to connect your high and low voice. Singing notes with ten tones between them also brings awareness of the breaks in our voices and how to smooth the breaks out. Practice a mere ten minutes daily. (He must be kidding!)

Such joy filled me whether I was good or bad at the task at hand. I was singing, singing, singing, singing. My proficiency at breathing musically and sticking with one musical idea grew over the course of the class.

Bobby balanced discipline with a willingness to take risks. In one breath he talked about internalizing his father's exacting standards. *Robert McFerrin, Sr., let singers get all the way through a song only one time. After that, he would stop them for every misplaced breath or ignored musical notation.* In the next breath, Bobby cut us slack if we couldn't learn his eleven-and-a-half-bar blues in five minutes. *Try it, he says. If you make a mistake, just say (à la Gomer Pyle), Golly, I messed up. Shoot.*

Twenty years of tension induced by performance anxiety seemed to leave my shoulders as I practiced my inflection on *shoot*. When we returned to learning the eleven-and-a-half-bar blues, I got it right away.

So maybe it really was okay that it took me thirty-two years to devote five consecutive days to developing the skills I needed to be a professional singer. Momma says I shouldn't count the first five years anyway. Still, I couldn't help wondering where I'd have been in relationship to my inner music if, like Bobby, I'd taken refuge under a master voice teacher's piano from the time I could.

Everywhere, we were singing. We created magical musical moments at lunch, chanting in the food lines. We practiced musical breathing together at the lake. Students from David Darling's course, "Music for Everybody," gathered around a picnic table in front of the dining hall to make music. There was a flute, a bell, a drum, several singers. I started a chant that goes round and round. My ecstasy was interrupted by an old white man from David's class who crouched down in front of me and started yelling in my face. He was probably trying to imitate me, and, bless his heart, even though I do believe in music for everybody, it was painful to be the object of his sonic projections.

I moved to the other side of the table to sing with the wooden bells rather than the flute. The old man followed me, yelling. In that moment, in that place, where I'd finally, finally focused on vocal mastery, I could handle only so much musical democracy. I left.

Sing at the same volume that you speak. Speaking-level singing gives you more room for dynamic control. Dynamics are intricately related to breath. Breathe fully, but only half of the air you inhale is available for singing. The other half = support. Keep it in reserve.

We sang in onesies and twosies. We played seriously with our voices, having more fun than I'd had since the last time I played master tournaments of jacks on my Momma's stone stairs. When Bobby sang bass under a melody I improvised, I knew, sure 'nough, that I was living and breathing in heaven.

We're sitting in a group of four singers, singing a simple two-note ditty that serves as a platform over which we practice soloing. The solos move in a clockwise circle. First, Bobby sings the bass melody for four bars. The group then sings eight bars of the melody in unison. Then, moving clockwise, we each solo for sixteen bars, then eight bars, then four bars, then two, then one bar four times around.

Bobby gives us instructions, and the counters among us freak. He tells us to trust that we can feel the time rather than count it. As we're singing, one woman starts to sing her solo louder, and the rest of us get excited and sing louder, too, drowning her out. Bobby points out our behavior. Tells us we have an option of singing dynamically as a group.

Shooooot.

We were constantly playing and working and spreading what we learned all over Omega. We sang a simple round at lunch, and several folks joined in. I got a massage, and the man who touched me ended by reading a Rumi poem translated by Coleman Barks. The poem began:

They try to say what you are, spiritual or sexual?

The caring with which the masseur touched me, a caring and quality of attention my husband was unwilling or unable to give at the time, mingled with the cells of me reawakened by the singing, singing, resurrected after so many years of forbidden being. I was vibrantly, achingly alive. The last lines of the poem moved immediately into song, and I sang them as I walked from the massage room to dinner:

> But we have ways within each other
> that will never be said by anyone.

Folks in the class wanted more and more information from Bobby about his plans in San Francisco and his life there and how did he do it and how could we do it like him. Folks in other classes at Omega wanted to know more and more information about what was happening in our class and how could they do what we were doing. We wanted, we wanted, we wanted more, more, more.

And I wanted so badly to talk with Bobby individually as the last day approached and I saw him talking individually to everybody in the class but me. I worried and wondered why he seemed to be avoiding me.

I must not have been good enough. It must have been because I am Black and tend to act bawdy around men who look like the men in my family. The NOcan'tDON'Tstops wouldn't shut up, and I sometimes cried myself to sleep at night because my self-doubts were so loud. I tried shouting them down: YEScanDOwillSO!

Bobby began one of our days together by having us choose a numbered piece of folded paper upon which he had written phrases we were then instructed to use as the basis for an improvisation. I choose number four. My phrase: "after orgasm." When it was my turn to improvise I poured myself on the floor and sang, "There is a melting at the meeting of our thighs."

The room got *hot*. Bobby said Yes! Someone accused Bobby of giving me that phrase on purpose. Remember, I said, we each drew a folded piece of paper randomly. Improvised poems began to pour out of me; poems proclaiming the source of singing and sensuality as one in the same. Remember, I said, we come into being in an action designed to bring us pleasure.

Play with four notes and only four notes. Play with the dynamics. Hang with only four notes for a while. Make subtle changes in the ways and sequence and tempo in which you sing them. Vary the amount of breath you allow to be audible as breath and how much you translate into tone. Treat these four notes as your most beloved home.

The last night of our week a friend from class, Caprice, and I jammed during a performance Bobby orchestrated. After we sang, I danced to the point of exhaustion. The moon was growing and growing, and I cried frequently at the mere thought of leaving and returning to what was my norm at home in California. At Omega, I felt more alive than I'd felt in years, since those daily rides on Red Horsey. A big swing, hanging from an ancient oak tree outside of the dining hall, swung me as I made love with the stars.

Still, at night, I felt like I'd burst open with what the week ignited. I prayed for the energy to be either transformed or, praying as my Momma so often prayed, taken away.

Shakti or no, no peace!

The master class ended as it began, with solo performances. True to Life, I didn't stick with one thing, but at least the trinity of elements in my offering were drawn from the same fountain and were well connected by musical breaths.

I began by singing "we have ways within each other" as I moved around the circle of singers, unsnapping the snaps of my jumpsuit to reveal my heart. I told the voices in whose presence some parts of me had been reborn that they left their tongue prints on my bones. I recited the poem sequence of "Bringings Up and Comings 'Round." I wanted my classmates and vocal master to hear deeply, into the depths of me, since it was unlikely that we'd all ever be together again.

And then I sang "Gratitude" (see page 16, in the Introduction), in a raucous thanksgiving for the days we'd spent together. When the workshop officially ended, Bobby and I had not yet managed to meet for my individual interview.

Outside of the main hall after the closing celebration, we sat on a bench and snatched a few frantic minutes, enough time for him to give me the name and number for Molly Holm, his assistant in the Bay Area. "She will know about the auditions for Voicestra," Bobby said. "Call her."

Folks milled around us in the chaos of packing and leaving and hugging good-bye. I knew that environment wasn't conducive for getting more feedback from Bobby on how to improve my vocal skills. While the week at Omega taught me that raw talent and desire were obviously not enough to make a profession of singing, I had no clue about where to turn to continue cultivating the vocal freedom that made me feel so alive.

But I did have Molly's number. And my closing performance contained every sublimated ounce of passion awakened by the week.

My mind soon shifted from my frustrating encounters with Bobby to the terror I felt at the prospect of taking my renewed sense of Shakti into my Momma's house for the visit I planned after Omega.

And the moon was growing and growing.

MUSIC OF GROWING THINGS

I WENT STRAIGHT FROM Omega to visit Momma, arriving more alive than I had been in her house since riding Red Horsey. *Full-out Shakti!* My body was red and singing, red and newly reborn by voice, by ear, into a heat and shining Momma could barely stand to see.

I came home red and new and still Momma's daughter, yes, but not only her daughter anymore. Shakti was ascendant. Momma sensed and did not like it. Her baby's voice was uncontrollably alive, and the vibing base of creative fire between my legs was alive, alive, alive. Nothing she did could douse me. I got so hot at Omega after a week of dynamic singing that I prayed for Life to take the passionate fire away, prayed for a stay of the vibrancy so deeply felt by all around that I attracted much unwanted sexual attention.

One week of singing with a vocal master, during his golden time, and I was born again. Voice and body reawakened together. Hallelujah! Practicing musical breathing for hours on end each day with a group of singers made the contrasting combat breathing I encountered in my Momma's house that much more painful.

Once again, Momma couldn't stand the sight of blood. I was thirty-two, too old and tall for her to hit the hot out of me, though her words and attitudes ripped at me relentlessly. She fought me fiercely in the soft place of my most powerful becoming. In my outbreath of Shakti, she fought me, in the place where bright shining all too often in the South of Momma's childhood led to more than one brown daughter's death. She called her fighting well intentioned. She only sought to guide me, only sought to protect her child.

Momma says, You feel unsettled. I ask, What do you mean by unsettled? I say, You have a judgment that what you feel moving inside of me is bad. She says she's not making a judgment but just has a feeling. She says she is not saying what she feels is bad, but that she is concerned. I try to hold back my judgment of her judgment. Whew. Whatever we're really doing while we're also talking is wearing me out. I say, it's okay for me to be in a changing place. I move my hands slowly and smoothly, in interlocking circles to show her my sense of the change going on within me. She shows me what she feels by moving her hands quickly, up and down, as if doing rapid-fire pétrissage along someone's spine. Watch my hands, Momma, I say. Watch my hands.

I was thirty-two and sitting with Momma at her kitchen table. In the lingo of improv, the kitchen table is *one*. One—the first beat in a measure, the tonic of a musical scale—is the beginning of the rhythmic pattern and melodic structure around which improvisations weave. One is the rhythmic sure thing, is the anchoring, is the known from which the unknown is entered. One is the rooting, is the ground through which vocal home is found when the mysteries of sound take us so far out that "in" seems to be a bad idea at best.

One is where the rest of the singers and players stay, while the improviser plays around. One is the season of reason and beginning, is the common place that graces us with courage to follow the sound within our hearts and inner other parts, into mysterious healing. With the kitchen table as one, I boldly insisted that Momma and I improvise new ways of relating to my full-out Shakti!

I tell Momma that the singing at Omega ignited something long dampened inside me. The singing made me shiny inside. What she felt was a freedom bringing her something I steeped in all week. I tell her about the birds who sang with us as we sang. I tell her about dancing in the growing moon with drummers trained by Babatunde Olatunji and feeling fully alive for the first time in years.

I tell Momma about opening my fuchsia jumpsuit as I sang my good-bye song at Omega, unsnapping the snaps that held together the cloth concealing my heart. I sing for Momma the song born of the poem that the masseur gave me, the poem of Rumi: They try to say what you are, spiritual or sexual. . . .

I tell Momma I want to live in a village where we sing such songs for weeks, regularly. I say I want the sonorous Life at Omega to be my day-to-day. Momma says, you got to fit into the culture. I say the culture is something I help create. Momma says, when in Rome, do like the Romans do. I say, Momma this ain't Rome. And if it is, then I was born here, I am Roman, too. How I do is part of how Romans do.

Momma says, you sing to make people happy. I say, I sing what Life bids me sing, surrender into the truth of the moment in absolute trust that what comes out of my mouth is what is called for, not what is inherited or thought to please. I do not sing to please anybody, not an audience, not myself. I sing to be the truth. I sing to dwell in love. I sing to simply be and sing freedom.

I was thirty-two and counting, fighting to convince Momma that my perception of Shakti as a blessing counts: respect it. Momma, powerful, sensed my young and growing parts, sought to instruct them with a mighty hand. We hurt each other in familiar ways.

As long as you in my house you do like I say do, Momma says. The way you do hurts. It's scary, Momma, I say. It makes me put up my shields. Yes, you do that, she says. You always resist me. Ever did. Ever have. What about Martin? she asks.

Martin doesn't have anything to do with what I'm feeling now, I tell Momma. We'll have to see if we can work some new way of relating out, but right now he's not responsive to me.

You got to wait your time with Martin, Momma says. I say, I can't trust what you say about Martin because I see how you related to Daddy and that doesn't seem so healthy to me. Well, Momma huffs, I have lived some, and my living has taught me you got to wait. I tell her life feels too tight when she says wait. I tell Momma all her waiting feels like stopping to me.

Momma is a storm. Momma is a sledgehammer. Momma feels like concrete walls around places in me that are growing. Momma's smothering silk intentions snatch my breath away. I fight Momma to keep breathing room around my Shakti newness.

A reunion of Momma's family happened to coincide with my visit following Omega. I was on the program to sing. Momma interrogated me about my plans, what songs I thought about offering. She was furious and frightened by my answering: I'll make something up.

She called what she was doing "warning" me. Most of these folks are not educated, she said. You sing to have them be happy. As we prepared to go, Daddy pulled me aside and told me what he thought I should wear to make Momma happy. I was angered by the ethic that making family members happy required sacrificing creative self-expression.

No wonder, that when I move to create I do so with fear and anguish, tooth and nail. When I move into the mystery of bringing something new into the world, into the view of others—women and men—I feel an almost overpowering impulse to put up my dukes, prepare to fight, snarl, and struggle. All past and future collaborators, be aware: creation as combat was part of my upbringing. Please forgive me.

Momma says my vibrancy is evidence of my being "high-strong" and having a hot behind. You came here like that, she says. She tells me I should talk to somebody who might help me grow out of my endowment of Shakti.

Ten thousand times I have endured Momma's retelling of why she sought to tear me from Shakti's creative shining. She said the only other person whose creative expression scared her like mine was my adopted Uncle Roe: a painter. His was a short and tragic life. Uncle Roe refused to live into his promise as a painter of portraits for rich, white patrons, much to the chagrin of his alma mater, the Philadelphia Academy of Fine Arts. He lived with us for a short time, painted in the basement, cooked meals for us, slept in the room where Daddy would usually store his drums. To encourage my singing, Uncle Roe gave me a drawing of Marian Anderson. Momma gave the drawing to his widow, after his untimely death.

Uncle Roe, genius, wouldn't paint white people. He died broke because he couldn't live on what he got to paint only Africans and American blacks. He was before his time, Momma always said, too in love with the lines and textures of African faces.

He was an artist and dead, an artist and torn up with drugs and grief. He wouldn't compromise and paint what the white people wanted, and so he suffered what Momma called unnecessary suffering. More than once, she vowed to my face that she would do her level best to make sure that what happened to Uncle Roe didn't happen to me. For the love of my life, she tore away the parts that wouldn't fit into what she perceived as acceptable society.

Sometimes it felt as though she held my essence in her hands like a thin piece of paper. She tore a large chunk off the bottom first; that was my sexuality. Another edge goes—too nappy. For the longest time, Momma insisted that I wear patent-leather-pressed-flat hair. Once I took Momma to the wig store to show her one of my favorite styles—Senegalese twists, snaking down the Styrofoam headform cut off at the neck. Momma almost passed out.

Slowly and quickly, she tore at bits of me that she thought too wild to survive. I spent nearly twenty years searching in my

Momma's eyes for approval of the torn parts. The parts she deemed acceptable felt too teeny-weenie to call a life. Somehow, in the fragmentation of what was and was not allowed, my ability to even sense self-wholeness was impaired. Momma's way of fitting me into "the culture" felt too narrow. Feeling her disapproval, even long-distance, felt like a breath-inhibiting stone on my chest.

Momma, beauty and devastation are accompanied by strong feelings. What I feel is natural, I say. I cry. I flame. Momma tries to douse the fires, dry up the tears. I must fight to feel. I take flight to feel. In the singing, the feeling is released, strengthened, freed, known and defended as worthy and real.

I looked in books for my missing notes and hard parts. The jagged edges of me were dangerously vulnerable. I sought medicine for what ailed me and found instead ointments, snake oils, this huckster, another pimp as I desperately searched for the self, the true Self that is closer at hand than this hand, closer to heart than this heart.

The parts that I've found, I've found by voice, a voice powerfully amplified by immersion for a mere week in a loved and struggled-for community devoted to vocal mastery. A community of folks, led by women and including many loving men, got me to Omega, where, for a week, I sang and sang and was fearlessly touched into healing by a gifted masseur, a white boy raised by a black woman.

Listen.

Listen to me, Momma, I say. The body cries. Our crying waters our freedom. The body laughs and sings. The body is an instrument of giving and receiving. The body is light and is water and is clay. Shakti is the body. The body fires up. The body is our ground, and a daughter's body is filled with thirty thousand Shakti-filled eggs, miracles, nestling in her ovaries.

> . . . all the people
> there will ever be
> inside
> before ever breathing a breath

The body aches, the body needs food and rest, needs water and acceptance. *The body composts, greens and sheds what falls away like brilliant leaves.*

The body cries. The body sings out sorrows, longings, triumphants, joys. The body hears what cannot be heard by ears. The body lives and, soon enough, dies.

Momma felt all this at her kitchen table and wanted to rein it in.

Momma's eyes look wild as she tells me that I am like a young calf, new in the spirit that claims me, wobbly and not yet strong enough to handle such strong energy flying offa my skin. Momma says she is simply trying to help me stand up. I ask Momma what a cow does for her calf and she says, stand by it. Then, I say, this is what you must do for me. Stand by, do not stifle, do not attempt to extinguish, do not try to twist, shape, and mold.

I sang Momma offa my spirit. I told her to let go of her hold. I dreamed a golden, luminously protective sphere around me that excised her grasping, well-intentioned, yet crushing Momma-hand off my throat.

Listen. Daughter Sister Mommas, listen.

It is another season now, another growing moon. We are now planting freedom while sitting at what I now call Momma's kitchen table altar. We are planting, with our tongues as spades and our Momma-Daughter bodies as our holy ground. We plant healing stories of growing things between us as we shell the black-eyed peas that surprised us with their ripeness in a nearby garden. We are planting a new singing as we harvest and prepare to put food away and to share what we know we cannot eat alone.

Sitting at Momma's kitchen table altar, we are planting and singing and harvesting our ways home.

DIVINE DAUGHTER SISTERS:
DAUGHTERS OF THE PUNA

Though we lived centuries and continents away, though we were Incan women, we shared with our Hebrew sisters the fact that our identities were shaped by place. We, too, came to our holy land after escaping oppression. Our suffering was at the hand of Spanish invaders who tried to destroy our gods and tax us for growing our food and breathing our air and bearing our children as our mothers had, as had their mothers before them.

Most of the Incan men were all too happy to follow the Spanish rule. Before the invaders came, possessions, names, and land were inherited in parallel lines: mothers to daughters, fathers to sons. In the Spanish world the men were all-powerful. Why should they listen to the voices of women, the Spanish asked our fathers, brothers, and sons, just because their fathers had listened, as had their fathers and theirs?

Line the invaders' pockets with coins that would otherwise put food on our tables? Pay Spanish taxes, pay homage to only their gods while we watch them destroy our own? Waste Life's gift of energy on trying to stifle the voices of our ancestors, women and men, singing in our bones?

No.

We took to the tablelands, we took to the high places, the *puna*. We took to the places few dare brave the journey to reach. We reached the puna by the grace of our ancestors, by the living of the old ones who did not forget. We remembered how to get to the safe places safely because the ones before us did not hold their tongues. They told us how to pray, they told us how to live in the rough places.

What, the Spanish way is more sacred than our own, than the ways that have kept us strong and living here forever? No. Do the waters and the mountains desert us like the Spanish demand that we forsake our fluids and our land? No. Will we pay their gods homage, pay the taxes that will keep their daughters fat while ours languish, pay our husbands and our sons more respect than they are due just because the Spanish say all men are deities, though they treat our men like trash?

No.

We take to the land that shares a name for a surface always in our domain: the table, the place that holds our food and our medicines; the table, where nourishment is prepared and presented and received.

We are the daughters of high table places. Sisters, Daughters of Jerusalem, hear our voices as we suffer and defy the religion born of your land.

We are Daughters of the Puna. We are wise and stubborn women. In our flight, we fight for our high place and to be wholly free.

lines   a-cross   the lines   Tell me what   you   see   Say-ing   we're

a-cross   the lines   a cross   the lines

a-cross   the lines   a cross   the lines

dow   zoom   ba dan   di din   doo   zoom   ba dan   di din

ba di di   ba di di   Ba de   da dum   bum bum   bum   ba de de   de   de   Ba   de   da dum   bum bum

Why sing? Why dare allow our hearts'
ringing sorrows, ringing joys, wonders,
ringing longings sound into song?

not free   to   reach   a-cross   the

a-cross the   lines   a-cross   the lines

a-cross the   lines

doo   zoom   ba dan   di din   di din   di doo   zoom   ba dan   di   din

ba de de   Ba de   dadum   bum bum   bum ba de de   de   de   Ba   de   da dum   bum

Excerpt from "Reach Across the
Lines," written by Rachel Bagby.
Copyright 1986 Breathing Music
ASCAP. Used by permission.

MANY SKINNED MIXED BLOOD

III.

I am a many skinned
mixed blood

African, not.

Cherokee
Scottish
East Indian

daughter
of mountains
of hot springs

Which one
is my tribe?

She
who
is
five tribes
in one

THIS IS A PRAISESONG.

Praises for and to African roots of all daughters' voices. Lucy, your sonorous bones, audible over millennia, unearthed from African soil, sing our cells home.

Scientists call you our most ancient elder. You, they say, were our actual Eve. You, they say, gave our species birth in all hues.

All praises, Lucy.

All praises to the Africans to whom I owe the brown in my skin's cherrywood coloring. To you who gave me a proud spread of nostrils to breathe well and sing well in heat, all praises.

Praises to the daughters of the daughters of the daughters who made me fertile dirt brown rhythm walking. Praises be to all who continually give me the gifts of playing the living, breathing polyrhythms dancing through our skins. Praises to you all for your mastery in speaking back beats. All, praises. All praises.

Praises to all who wept and sang to bear me. You who survived brutal middle passages, praises. All praises due to our black root, Lucy, mother of all daughters' pumping blood drums.

Praises to the red root of Great-Great-Great-Aunt Lula, woman who helped birth innumerable daughters. Cherokee, mixed blood Aunt Lula, receive these praises for all the LifeDeathLife that you balanced and knew.

For accepting my four-year-old Momma as midwifing student, praises, all praises, Aunt Lula. Praises for how you taught and helped my Momma remember: with the cycles of seasons and with singing and with prayer.

For teaching her where to go to dig what root when and why, Aunt Lula, receive these praises. For the women's remedy of bark from the longleaf pine's sunrise side, I sing your praises. For offering teething children catnip tea sweetened with wild bees' honey, praises. For the beeswax rubbed on to soothe children's teething-torn gums, all praises, Aunt Lula, all praises.

Praises for holding vast property, gardens, and woodlands in balance, in the ways of your people. Praises for your skill in caring for hundreds of families and several generations. Praises for being a mixed blood who honored and passed on Earthma's gifts in the ways of our Cherokee kin. For the giving spirit with which you cherished these red-rooted gifts, three-greats-Aunt Lula, blessings, all praises.

Praises for and to the Scottish man Great-Grandmom Liz nursed and married, Great-Granddad Jennings. All praises for breaking your family's tradition of owning other human beings, all praises. For winning Great-Grandmomma's freedom, and giving her land to call her own, praises. Praises for honoring Great-Grandmom Liz and her wisdom about what to plant how and when.

Great-Granddad Jennings, for sending all of your daughters, including my Grandmomma Eva, to college, praises. Praises for giving Grandmom Eva your Celtic harp and the spirits with which to play it. Praises. From the daughter of your daughter's daughter, receive these praises for your white-rooted gifts.

Praises to you for a legacy of bodacious freedom, Elizabeth Minerva Simianne Texas Jennings. Great-Grandmom Liz, all praises. For your hundred and four years of living, and how you lived and died, praises.

Great-Grandmom Liz, praises for knowing what was coming long before it arrived, praises. For our legacy of food sovereignty, of knowing what to plant during which growing moon, praises. For the ways in which you prayed behind closed doors and with dancing, your heavy skirt hitting the floor as you whirled your prayers, Great-Grandmomma Liz, all praises.

Mom Mountain, covered with sweet chaparral, manzanita, and rattlesnakes, receive all praises. Praises for the powerful little sisters you hold in your lap, the hot springs, all praises. For your healing clay, berries, and fig juice. For your silences under clear nights' screaming stars. For whispering "Bringings Up and Comings 'Round" poems into my thirtieth-birthday ears, praises. For the new poem form "10." For sending me home to revive the *daughter / of daughter* stories my human Momma and I both required to fully live, all praises, Mom Mountain, all praises.

African, Cherokee, Scottish, East Indian, mountain, and hot springs elders, all praises.

BLESSED IS SHE

BLESSED, BLESSED IS SHE whose being knows the multiplicity of all daughters' every cell. Blessed is she who dwells in an ease of loving all beings when battling kin would claim her as only their own.

I pray to be such a daughter.

Blessed, blessed is she who has lived beyond definitions of *us* and *them,* of the way we are and they are, of external enemies internally blended in her very blood. Whom shall she mistreat, call stranger?

Blessed is she who cultivates the power of clearly seeing how we tear at ourselves even as we are blinded to the fact that we are ourselves and one another. Blessed, blessed is she whose breath, intention, tone, rhythm, and repetition help to heal our ism schisms without and within.

Oh, Life, make of me such a daughter.

Her ears are tested by what she hears of the hatred hurled at the others folks think are not present in her presence. Her tongue is tested in the company of those who confide in her as "one of us" without realizing she is also a daughter of "them." Her eyes are tested when some of "us" with whom she shares blood cannot see her because of her appearance, her skin. Her heart is tested, tempered to be compassionate toward the hatred and the longing, for the suffering and the delusion, for the anger and the greed she notices without and within.

Many skinned, mixed blood daughters know the sorrow of being asked to sing allegiance to only one world while being so filled with many, many voices that rarely feel fully embraced by her human communities.

Choose, choose, choose, choose, choose, each side says without saying why this one hates Blacks, another hates descendants of Europeans, that one hates all Europeans except Jews, another hates her own rhythmic being because it is hated by the others with lighter skins.

Blessed, blessed is this daughter's power, this daughter's challenge, this daughter's calling, this daughter's falling down and getting up and falling down and getting up again:

To simply dwell at home in all her bloods and skins. To be home, to free home, to liberate home, in all her cells from mixed legacies of hatred.

To be friend with all who are truly friend. To know that the features of all faces and colors of all skins cover infinite treasures.

To know that love and anger comes in all hues, that all peoples suffer, and that among all peoples are those who aspire to realize the promise of peace.

To know and eschew the wages of ill will. To stand up, even if shaky, and say, "This hurts me; let's not contract in hatred today."

To know that to choose always to give voice to only one voice of herself is to somehow lie. And to know also that to be called to serve in a particular voice can be a blessing.

To know that there is no always, *it,* right way, or being.

To dance today and tomorrow to compose a song, and the day after that, a poem, and the next day to awaken in a dream that screams her into clearer being.

To love Life's great wheel turning; to know in all its colors there are fires, bright as little candles on each spoke's turning tip.

At the bottom of Life's turning, each spoke dips into water and emerges covered with tears bright as jewels that then burst into flames; then Life swirls her around again, toward the apex of the great wheel's turning, her colors ever changing . . .

To know that she is ever changing, Life, the movement of the great wheel, the colors and the dance, the burning tongues.

Blessed, blessed is she who knows and faces her challenges with the quiet stillness of the drummer's daughter. Blessed is she who grows and tends the kindred voices of Life's many tongues.

So bless me, please, Life. So bless all daughters.

REACH ACROSS THE LINES

WOMEN OF SPIRIT, women of power from many blood-lines and of many skins gathered to tell one another our stories of social actions and strategies for Life. Petro paved the way for our gathering. We met in Texas at an estate called Stonehaven. We were told that the woman financing our meeting was the daughter of an oil tycoon.

We were activists; college presidents; film and theater artists; dancers; independent scholars of ancient goddess religions and three thousand years of racism; composers; vocalists; professors of religion, women's studies, Native American oral literature and crafts, sociology, and history; philanthropists; community leaders; journalists; healers; publishers of academic journals; spiritual mavericks, pagans, Christians, Buddhists, Wiccans, Yorubas, spirited and politically engaged women.

We were from Sri Lanka, El Salvador, England, and many regions, many nations within the United States. Our bloodlines and skin included Jewish, Spanish, Scottish, Asanti, Cherokee, Fulani, Celt, WASP, and many daughters in between.

We gathered to deepen our understanding of the nexus of spirituality and politics. How could the two be truly separate? I wondered then, wonder now. All politics are engaged in one spirit or another, in the breath of hatred or of reconciliation, devoted to raping or restoring the Earth.

We gathered in response to the political activities of the religious right. We gathered to strategize with the women among us who were worn out by violent responses to their direct actions for women's liberation, peace, spiritual freedom, economic justice, and ecological integrity. We were called together to name and name again how we lived spirit and how our spirits informed our politics. We gathered to explore the marriage of wise breath and public action.

The food was good. Stonehaven was isolated enough to afford us quiet evenings. The women were funny and smart. We laughed a lot. We disagreed with one another passionately. We fought and made up.

As we went around to introduce ourselves, I sang and spoke of my work with my Momma, greening the working-class North Philly neighborhood she still called home. I talked of our multiple gardens, children's programs, and rehabilitated houses; our practices of prayers and the dreams guiding our actions. I talked about how Momma's project made good use of my newly acquired knowledge, contacts, and skills the summer after my first year of law school. I talked about how the organization was my net when I came home three years later on a bus, mind and life shattered.

I sang.

The colored women met on our own, and when we gathered together in the larger group one white woman asked what we'd talked about.

Elena Featherston, the author and filmmaker I have to thank for being invited to the gathering, answered with some version of, "That's for us to know and you to find out." I chimed in, "We didn't discuss what we would disclose to the larger group or keep to ourselves. But I feel safe in saying that we spent the time loving ourselves rather than talking about you."

Both Elena and I spoke truly in response to the question. But being my Momma's daughter and the spirit with which I responded to the request for a report from the colored girls contributed to my being invited to the planning meetings for what would later become "WomanEarth: A Feminist Peace Institute," so named by Luisah Teish.

WomanEarth focused on the cultivation of what in 1986 was a new movement, ecofeminism. The name was not well known then in either feminist or ecological circles. We were trying to construct or recognize the theory of what we were beginning to notice of our lives—how our concerns for women and for living systems led to public actions. Ecology, feminism, spirituality, common differences, and public action were the spokes of our circle of concern. Common differences included analysis of ism schisms and economic oppressions that sabotaged our effectiveness.

WomanEarth meetings were smaller and enjoyed parity between women of color and white women. We were planning a meeting to be held at Hampshire College in Amherst, Massachusetts. Parity was essential. When Barbara Smith, cofounder and editor of Kitchen Table Press, was asked to participate, she conditioned her involvement on parity.

We traveled all around the country, meeting, planning. We met once at Grace Paley's house in New York, once at a camp in New England, another time at Stonehaven. The cost for all our travel and activity was paid for by our sponsor, Oil's Daughter.

At the first Stonehaven meeting, one of the sponsor's female relatives ate lunch with us all. She told me in a most gentle southern drawl that she did not nor would she ever see us as equals. I didn't think to thank her in the moment for acknowledging my superior musical or oratory skills, which outsang anything she'd offered. I knew she was also a lawyer, but I didn't ask her where she went to law school or where she had ranked in her class. I didn't wonder if she recognized that my youth and beauty were superiorities she could never, never equal.

Feigned arrogance aside, something inside of me knew that her whiteness and money and the life both afforded her were the roots of her confession. My appetite left, as did all interest in continuing our conversation. What was there to say to someone so blatantly aligned with inequity?

Our sponsor at least aspired to another allegiance. Her aspiration was put to the test on the third day of one planning meeting when we began discussing the other women we thought to invite. The sponsor mentioned someone who must be there. *Must?* we asked her. Who is this woman, and what has she done, and what does she do in the world?

The sponsor sputtered something about not having to justify or defend her choices of participants. We reminded her that we were operating as equals, that each of us had a voice about who to invite and that we were asking her, as each of us had been asked, to give more information about the women we proposed to enter into dialogue with us.

The sponsor exploded, "If you people won't do what I want, then I'll find somebody else who will!"

Ah, we discovered, we were merely her servants, not her equals. We were merely invited to do her will, follow her dictates, keep her happy. The nappy-headed girls were simply to say yes ma'am, yes ma'am to the sponsor's desires. We were not really collaborating. We were being paid to serve one rich white woman's vision rather than collaboratively create a vision we each could call our own.

Ah, we forgot, the moneyed call the shots. Our experience and thinking and connections and abilities were not considered by our sponsor as equally important as her cash. And if we would not do her bidding, well, then, she would not attend the party, and she would start another more in line with what she thought would save the world.

She called herself a devotee of the gift economy. But it seemed that hers was a gift with strings.

Anger rang around the circle in gasps, clinched eyes, and arms crisscrossed under breasts. One woman said out loud, "What I feared was the case was true. You are in charge, and we'll work together just fine as long as we serve you."

Our illusion of equity was shaken by the outburst of owner-class ethics. The sponsor's tantrum threw us into the dynamics of classes and cultures clashing, again.

Again, white and rich supremacy reared her voice, again, again. Once again, the hand of many skinned and mixed blooded class legacies slapped our faces, even in the midst of a meeting with the best of intentions. Again, neither our breath nor our intention, neither the tone we set with parity between colored and noncolored girls nor our longing for freedom was enough to prevent the rhythms of injustice from repeating themselves in our collective behavior. Again, when the po' and colored girls insisted on collaborating with equal power, the rich white girl went into a huff.

In the midst of the turmoil, the pattern we struggled to keep breathing through sang itself to life in my ears as "Reach Across the Lines." The bridge of the song gave voice to the moment:

Fire answers fire
Pain answering pain
Memory and desire
Colliding again

The sponsor exploded out of her desire and expectation and memory of having her ideas and desires met with yes ma'am, yes ma'am. Many of us had bloodlines and skins of people she was raised to rule. Yet we'd all put aside weeks of our lives to fly all over the country to meet one another—*meet*—and see how we could gather our energies into a vivifying movement.

We remembered our historical places. The pain accompanying our attempts to step outside the dictates of those places fueled feelings of betrayal, anger, old hatreds. Our desire to bring women together to support one another's efforts for our lives and the Earth collided with our conditioning. *Again. Again. Again.*

And I sang:

Terrible the freedom
Unbearable the lives
If in this moment—eye-to-eye
Each of us dares to reach across the lines

We managed to extend ourselves collectively so we could talk about the dynamics threatening to undermine our efforts. The moment presented a perfect opportunity to prepare for the kinds of fireworks we were sure to experience at the gathering we planned. While "Reach Across the Lines" did not have the power to transform completely the dynamics it named, it at least helped a few hearts in the room stay open to the possibility that we could do things differently.

The sponsor's behavior could be named without demonizing her. The rest of us could recognize our accumulated resentment over the persistent injustice we now tussled with, again, and could vigilantly guard against allowing long-term resentments to harden into hatred. We could use our rift as a perfect opportunity to articulate the values and collaborative agreements we wanted to practice instead.

We could, in a word, heal: receive our pain as the evidence of what divided us and as a brilliant indicator of its antidote, behavior that would reconcile each to each and each to the whole.

We only partially lived up to the promise of the moment that birthed "Reach Across the Lines." The conference was held as planned, though the sponsor never attended another of our planning meetings. Nor did she attend the conference, but she did pay for it, as promised. I can't say that I blame her. She would have had a hard row to hoe, as my Momma would say. I still fantasize that one day she and I will follow the guidance of the chorus to "Reach Across the Lines":

> *Keep on reaching*
> *Across the lines*
> *Let your eyes meet mine*
> *Across the lines, across the lines*
> *Now let's take the chance*
> *To dance a brand new dance*
> *And reach*
> *Reach across the lines*

DAUGHTER OF MOUNTAIN

L ET ME TELL YOU how Mom Mountain redaughtered me after I
was raped.

When I cried out for a reason to keep living, Mom Mountain answered with pictures that showed me she understood what I was
going through, showed me that the Earth endured multiple takings,
too, in the forms of despoiled rivers, strip-mined land, and clear-cut
ancient forests. Mom Mountain showed me the devastation other
forms of Life endured and how, with all its might, Life continued.

Mom Mountain showed me soiled rivers rolling on and flowers in
clear-cut fields still growing; *have mercy.*

Imagine my surprise, as I stood in the wilderness—alone and in
shock—to feel comforted by a mountain, something I was raised to
consider unmoving and hard. Yet Mom Mountain had a spirit older
and much softer than stone. Something of deep feeling dwelled in
the high rugged place, something that witnessed my taking, something that legend says the native Pomo tribe recognized as sacred before Mom Mountain was "discovered" by folks made rich by gold.

Some softness of Mom Mountain's being held me, rocked me.
Some air breathing itself through me redeemed the surrender forced
by a man; it filled the holes rammed into me with songs, with
prayers, with beauty.

Mom Mountain showed me how Life endured destruction at the
hands of humankind. She spoke in the languages of beauty and horror. She showed me pictures of creation juxed against those of destruction. She showed me how places she knew were ripped into and
how beauty grew out of her lap and how waters laughed down her

slopes. Mom Mountain gave me hope that I could also heal and thrive.

When I say that I am the daughter of Mom Mountain and her hot springs, I mean that many of the songs I sing and that others find so nourishing were born in her lap. I mean that she seemed to rock me back into Life following the death of identity and bodily sovereignty that rape can be. The songs born of my arising are as much her grandchildren as they are my creations. For these gifts, I thank Mom Mountain.

Since that time, I have had friends tell me that in their traditions, the mother is the first ground against whom we kick. Well, then, Mom Mountain was my second ground, and she redaughtered me well. For this gift, I praise her name.

In some ways Mom Mountain came to know me better than any of my other mothers, even better than the one who gave me birth. She spoke to me in a picture language that easily breathed directly into song. She taught me an integrity I did not learn from other mothers. She helped me understand how the twin beings of beauty and devastation are continually living and breathing side by side. She taught me that running away from my challenges did no good and that there was no place to hide from Life Itself.

Her broad thighs strengthened mine. Many, many songs were born on and in her. The roots of Life-revering creativity were her greatest gifts and the foundation of everything she taught me. Groves of madrone and manzanita trees were her church and her school. And her living community was populated equally with rattles of deadly snakes and the juicy fruit of fig trees.

Mom Mountain was and is herself. There was nothing hidden of her vastness of being, though there were many mysteries. I didn't need to go to any books for interpretations of many of her deepest lessons. She didn't point me away from myself but rather showed me how to learn by emulating other forms of Life. And the sweetness she offered did not cost me my soul.

To fully receive what Mom Mountain offered required me to face my own greed and delusions. Like my human Momma, Mom Mountain did not and could not protect me from the greed and cruelty of humans. She stood in silent witness to many takings and kept giving, kept helping me repair what was then my life on her skin.

I was blessed to be daughtered by Mom Mountain, to be comforted by her, and, yes, to be tried. Her incline slowed down and strengthened my stride. I walked her tempering inclines every day, and the effort strengthened my lungs. My limbs were made muscular by walking to Mom Mountain's secret places, places reachable only by foot.

To be redaughtered by Mom Mountain was a blessing filled with songs. "Of the Divine," one of the songs that won me a place in Bobby's master class at Omega, was born there, as was "Grandmothers' Song." Both the music and redaughtering I received from Mom Mountain were featured in the Emmy Award–winning documentary, *Dialogues with Madwomen.*

And when it was time for me to leave to gather the stories of women in my family, Mom Mountain sent me home.

ANCESTRAL ASSIGNMENT

Find our stories
Speak our stories alive

Stories as blood
As liver

Great-Great-Great
Aunt Lula
Dances my cartilage

Great-Grandma Liz
On my Lips
Sings

THE WOMEN IN YOUR FAMILIES have stories they may never be able to tell you in words, yet you'll live them. Listen for their unsaids in all the ways they respond to your body: passion, envy, anxiety, approval, critique. Hidden in their eagerness to raise you up straitjacket proper, hidden in the ways they let you fall, are longings that they try to rename with your name.

Find them. Find their unsaid stories, or those stories will eat you alive.

There in your body's health or discomfort—women's stories. There in your hidden questions—many stories waiting to be sung.

There in your female relatives' closed lips and unspeaking eyes lie what you may sometimes feel you're dying of—

—Phantoms of untold daughters' stories. Love them. Love these longing-to-be-heard unsaids. Love them into being sung freely, and then listen to the soundings of your life.

DIVINE DAUGHTER SISTERS: DOMESTIC WISDOM

This morning I made the mistake of turning the front burner on under a Pyrex pie plate. The dish rested where my teakettle normally would. I turned on the burner I normally would to boil water, which I would then usually pour over my morning tincture of vitex and lady's mantle to burn off the alcohol. This daily tincture I take to modulate my hormonal balance and help prevent the growth of a uterine fibroid.

As I noticed the glass dish resting on the burner, I thought, oh-oh, this glass is not meant to handle that kind of intense, direct heat. I moved to turn the heat off and remove the glass from the burner. As I held the dish, it exploded into big and needle-little bits.

I thought of daughter sisters the world over. In that moment I was grateful not to have young, flesh-and-blood daughters in the house. Then I wondered, if I lived with younger daughters of my womb, would I have already learned a motherly attention that would have known not to put a Pyrex pie plate on the stovetop?

As the glass exploded, I let out a high-pitched *whoo*. I felt a tiny shard of glass bounce off my face. I noticed little pieces of glass scattered all around the stove and the sink and as far out in the eastern corner of the room as the kitchen drum (where any other woman would have her kitchen table) and as far as the water cooler in the kitchen's western corner.

Then I walked out. I noticed I was not bleeding and that I was very lucky. I walked out into the vestibule to sit down on the steps and get my nerves together. My husband was still asleep upstairs. I was surprised he heard neither the shattering nor my sound. I was surprised and a little scared that such danger could pass unnoticed. I sat down deliberately to calm myself and my wildly drumming heart. I noticed the racing slow down as I imagined opening the bottom of my feet and the top of my head to release the adrenaline going every which way inside of me. I visualized opening up my body and becoming first a stream of healing rain, then a rushing river with water running throughout and cleansing me.

Then I went back to clean up what was shattered.

Somewhere in all of this there were many thoughts of daughter sisters. I thought of how our daughterly lives are often lived in the midst of shattered yet somehow still luminous traditions. As I cleaned up shards of glass, I remembered that in matrilocal cultures the locale of the mother determines where the married girl lives and that a continuity and aesthetic maturity of designs is evident in the pottery shards. I remembered that where the daughters move into the husbands' compound, the pottery shards show a hodgepodge of designs.

I remembered the wisdom of the nearby herbs passed along from woman to woman for generations—the healing herbs, the beauty-accenting herbs, the herbs that clear the arteries of hardness and the heart of inflexibility. I remember an elder sister teaching me the herbs that bring healing visions and the ones that take destructive rigidities away. All this I remembered in the midst of shattered glass.

I remembered this as I picked up bits and pieces of glass and noticed the seemingly infinite microscopic pieces still to retrieve, pieces visible less by their substance than by their shining. I planned my strategy for cleaning up broken glass without getting cut and for protecting others who would enter this now-danger-filled room. As I finessed the shards of what was once whole and used to cook nourishment but now could hurt us, I thought of daughter sisters.

I thought about how much of our daughterly lives are like the heat that made the Pyrex so hot it could explode. Our voices and daughterly stories can heat something up inside of us until it is so hot that our lives as we now live them can shatter all around us, and then we need to find other containers in which to live and receive nourishment.

The shattered container was on the stovetop because my husband had left it there the night before, after using it to heat my castor oil pack, which I place nightly over my pelvis to energize that part of us that I call Ms. V. and to discourage fibroids from growing. I noticed how something that was used to make medicine more powerful could, in a moment's unawareness, explode into infinite pieces.

Remember this, daughter sisters.

Learn with me about the need to become aware of what too much heat and light can do to the vessels of clarity that our voices can be. And learn of the powers of domestic wisdom: liberating knowledge that our day-to-day experiences with so-called women's work allow us to perceive and voice.

All this I thought of, daughter sisters, as I carefully picked up the slivers of glass. I put on oversized, heavy, orange rubber gloves to protect my hands as I moved inch by inch over the floor with a garment brush and dustpan, sweeping up glass shards.

The day called for more care each step of the way. After sweeping both the floor and the edge of the sink, I used my bare hands to pick up large shards off the stove. Some were shaped like bits of a monochromatic stained-glass window, just that intricate, that deliberately cut. Others looked as though a mere glance could send them splintering off into infinitely tinier pieces. These I picked up and bagged with care.

I thought of daughter sisters. I thought of these shards as part of our daughterly brilliance, the stories we seek and sing. And I took care lest my wanderings in the webs of metaphor snatched away too much attention, snatched me a disastrous second away from what my fingers needed to know of touch: this much pressure, and the glass makes it safely from the stove into layers of paper. Too little or too much pressure, and I risked receiving more colorful lessons from broken glass.

The large shards removed, I returned to work on the smaller shards with swish broom and dustpan and gloves. Tinkling signaled errant shatterings making their way to the floor. Fingers, eyes, ears, and a careful attention born of a subtle sense of fear all worked together slowly, carefully. There were shards in the steam pan on the back burner, kitty-corner to the one that heated up the glass. Shards had made their way into every cup and dish drying on the dish rack. Everywhere I looked there was evidence of shattering, and I wondered how I could safely gather it all up and render it harmless, wondered at the beauty of brokenness as I used the sponge to get what slipped away from fingers, from swish broom, from rubber gloves, and saw the sponge begin to shimmer, shimmer with bits of glass.

I worked until tiring of the attention required. As I rested, I heard my sweetie start barefoot down the stairs to greet me and gather me back into bed for our morning ritual of heart-time. I rushed to warn him to be careful.

I write to warn you, daughter sisters. Remember to take care with the heat and the freedom your voices are becoming. Remember to be full of care with the fires of our beings, fires that our singing and speaking heat up. And if we are blessed to meet each other eye-to-eye one day, please remind me, daughter sisters, to carefully tend our tender and fierce freedom.

PRAISESONG OF TREE-LEAF WOMAN'S FREEDOM

Tongued spontaneously, freely spoken or sung
Your experiences of freedom recorded by others
Preserved by yet other daughters centuries later
In another land

The tongues of Tantric women from India are long
Reach over quite a few bumpy places
Okay, we call them mountains
But what is a mountain to Life

Your voices ring into Tibet
Because the huntress Padmalocanā
Wrote your freely spoken, freely
Given freedom songs sung out loud
Down

Through the ages your songs are still singing insights
Into our almost twenty-first century ears

Praises, Tree-Leaf Woman, Praises of your song!

Who speaks the sound of an echo?
Who paints the image in a mirror?
Where are the spectacles in a dream?
Nowhere at all—that's the nature of mind!

—Translated by Miranda Shaw

BECOMING VIBRALINGUAL

A s we live and breathe, we already express polyrhythmic vibrations day and night. Our hearts cyclically pump blood throughout our bodies. We breathe in rhythms modulated by our emotions: now in the 4/4 of a well-established meditation, now in a waltz, now a tango, now in the torrid breath of ancient fertility rites. Some say that each of our organs has a cycle of contraction and expansion. Every moment, our skins dance an unseen yet real undulation as they regulate our temperatures and eliminate waste.

Being vibralingual is a physiological fact of our living and breathing. A flash of flying color outside my writing-room window catches my eye, flits yellow from lower, lighter green branches to higher, darker green limbs. Imagine wholeheartedly giving our tongues to powers of color. Imagine speaking a vivifying green or singing a soothing blue to someone who loves you.

Imagine being consciously vibralingual.

What we call green can be measured as a wave of light oscillating at approximately 550 to 554 nanometers per cycle. Our ability to perceive and measure green, a rhythmically rooted perception of light, says something about our potential to be consciously vibralingual.

The fact that light can be measured, and that we can translate colors into numerical representations, or rhythms, of light, implies that light also can be translated into something we could sing or drum out on a taut belly. The possibility of translating light into body music says something about our potential for becoming vocally vibralingual.

Music waves. Light waves. Water waves. We are oceans walking; 78 to 82 percent of our bodies is composed of water and space— mediums through which light and sound become perceptible.

We live within an infinity of cycles, measured, measurable, and immeasurable. To become conscious of them, of their music, of the fact that Life is both drummer and drum, is to become vibralingual. How many such rhythms, you might ask, do we have to be conscious of and articulate in before we can call ourselves fully vibralingual?

Let us put such calculations aside for the moment; even though *in numbers we trust* is one of our cultural mottoes. Yes, daughters need economic and political power, powers predicated on numbers, on the measurable. Yes, most of us need jobs to earn money for rent or mortgage or to buy, rather than grow, our food. Ah, women, again and again the commercialization of life stands in direct opposition to living by natural cycles, requires the hurried-up pace made possible by the mechanized and measurable: r.p.m., m.p.h., and what my friend Patrick Nicoletti calls Cartesian slave bracelets, a.k.a. watches.

Let us lay all that aside for now. Let us focus instead on the tongues of our inner knowing, the still small voices inside that are often discounted because they are too wise to subject themselves to our measured intentions. Let us give tongue to that which operates outside of our attempts at dispassionate control. Let us imagine how being fully vibralingual could restory our lives.

To know while we are listening to certain instruments that we are relaxing, that we are waxing into ecstasy, waning out of stress: this is to become vibralingual. To practice discerning similar transformations in the songs or words of daughter sisters, our parents, lovers, certain places, certain sights—a well-lit populated street at night, the patch of wild park in the midst of the city, the silence of a wild place punctuated by the laughter of a creek—is to become vibralingual. Pay attention long enough, with a liberating quality of mind, to relationships between sounds and sights—expressions of Life's oscillating, changing, vibratory realities—and you will eventually become vibralingual.

I have spent many vibralingual moments in Grace Cathedral, in the name of the sacred feminine. Some of these moments have been harmonious, others have not. I am remembering a less-than-harmonious meeting to organize the beginning of the "Renaissance of the Sacred Feminine Conference," hours before Grace's doors were scheduled to open. Members of the Bay Area Lesbian Women's Chorus were joining me to sing "I Am a Full Woman," while I encouraged the congregation to sing along. Rather than change the lyrics to accommodate men's voices or improvise another part for them, I suggested inviting the men present to bask in the women's powerful self-affirmation.

One of the conference organizers responded with an impassioned statement about the sacred feminine being in both women and men and not being limited to one gender.

"What if the Goddess herself appeared and said to change the lyrics? What would you do then? Did you understand me?" he asked, as though speaking in a language other than the English we both considered one of our native tongues.

I understood him to be offended by my suggestion that the men practice receiving women's expression of full womanhood. The action of receptive listening is deemed one of the most cherished qualities of the feminine in Western cultures. From his tone of voice and heated response, I gathered that my colleague thought I was excluding men from affirming their sacred feminine qualities. On the contrary, I was asking men to fully embody divinity's cherished receptivity. I felt misunderstood.

"Well, if the Goddess"—which one? I wondered—"appeared, then perhaps I'd consider changing the words," I said.

I neither changed the words nor made the announcement. Whosoever felt moved to sing along with us sang.

The evening ended with Zuleikha, an exquisite dancer, decked out in white, twirling on white marble, flanked by three white men. The scene was white on white on white on white on white, with a man sitting behind Zuleikha, in the middle of the sanctuary, on an elevated, velvet-covered seat.

I was not about to let this monotone image of sacred femininity be the last one to rest in people's eyes that evening. I asked Karolyn van Puttan, another Black woman, vocalist, and scholar/practitioner of vocal healing, if she'd stand with me behind the high altar, in visual contrast to all the whiteness in the sanctuary below. Even though she had already changed into overalls, Karolyn said a great big *yes!*

With Karolyn and me, brown entered the picture—brown and another angle of perception. I was dressed in yellow; Karolyn's overalls were blue. We stood there silently with our hands folded in prayer. With our bodies, an Earth-colored vibe entered the picture, and, in our subversion, we gave the visual presentation of the sacred feminine a much-needed depth.

The next day I coordinated a collective improvisation entitled "Creativity and the Sacred Feminine." The other players: David Darling, a cellist; Zuleikha, dancer; Karolyn, my sister in voice and overalls from the night before; and Geoffrey Gordon, a tabla player. We each had fifteen minutes in which to express elements of our work that related to the sacred feminine.

David opened our session by improvising on his warm, brown alto of a cello. He held his cello firmly between his thighs as he stroked its strings with a bow, a length of wood graced by taut horsehair. The pressure, the caress of horsehair against metal strings, shape-shifted into audible light. David's cello sang, and we were soothed by its singing.

Geoffrey, the tabla player, shy of speaking, spoke of loving the rhythms he played and how he learned to play them. Lightning quick and intricate, his tabla playing was a many-fingered thing. Were his beloved rhythms divine? Was his playing feminine? Who was to say? Whose words would be acceptable as truthful, as a trustworthy judgment?

Zuleikha moved us with her stories and with her Kathak-trained feet. Kathak, a rhythmic, classical storytelling-dance form of northern India, amplifies the fact that our every step drums the Earth.

Karolyn led us in ahhing our hearts open. Over and over she encouraged us to open our bodies and ah as she sang over our ahhing and we were opened. For ten minutes we ahhed while Karolyn sang. In the ahhing, I, too, opened. Something of me rested. I loved this ahhing rumbling opening the warm in the center of my chest, my heart. We sang ah-open, wide open long enough for something to shift into collective sighs when we were done.

Then it was my turn. Not knowing what I would do when I got up, I got up. The night before my prayers had been simple: to be present with what was, to give voice clearly, purely to what was called for.

I began with questions. As I turned to the right, to my brother artists sitting behind me, I asked out loud—is it feminine? Then I turned to my sister artists and asked, is it divine?

"What did you come for?" I asked. I spoke of my longing for a community devoted to the sacred feminine. I spoke of this longing, a longing that dragged me three thousand exhausted miles from my New England home to the beloved northern California of my young adulthood.

I confessed that, en route, so many tasks claimed my mind that within hours of arriving in Berkeley I ran into an indestructible Volvo. My rental car was rendered inoperable by the encounter. I also injured my back. The Volvo lost just a bit of detailing on its right fender.

What had each of us damaged or sacrificed to be together, in the name of the sacred feminine? What longing, what unmet someNONthing did we want goodly enough in our lives to spend so much time and money and so many hours sitting on hard church pews? As I spoke with exasperation and passion, my shawl hurled itself out into the congregation. Its whirl of soft, silk colors—green, silver, midnight blue, turquoise, golden yellow—hurt no one yet seemed to shock us all awake.

The shawl's vibe changed the vibe of the room.

I put down the microphone, an artificial amplifier of tongues, knowing that I could be heard in the back without it. Opera singers would be appalled at what my voice then did, powered as it was by a passion bordering on an anger too intense to care for vocal cords. An unnamed, in-the-moment intensity of emotion raised my fists up and had me stomping my bare feet on the floor, whomping the air, saying that the ways we were living were killing us and so much more Earthwide. Was our way of living divine? Was it feminine?

A rant poured out of my mouth: You would think we didn't recognize our reliance on the cycles in Life's vibratorium, given our collective disregard for safeguarding their continued, natural existence rather than relying, instead, on what we make of what is cut, on the bleached and then green-colored pieces of dead tree skin we call money.

Fists up, I admonished all present, myself included, to stop it; stop the destruction. If we were truly devotees of the creative, feminine, sacred, then we needed to stop living in ways that wiped out so many lives. This outburst, in defense of Life, burst out unrehearsed, out of my cherrywood-colored, breasted, improvising form.

Then I sat down.

Then we entered a collective improvisation. I start us off by singing long tones. Karolyn harmonized with me in minor intervals. The other instruments joined in: cello, tabla. Zuleikha moved to the front of the pulpit that served as our stage and started dancing low to the floor. What we made was made in that moment and made of it and of all that has gone before. Our singing was a wail and a groan, grown into extended, women's tones. Karolyn started a new melodic line, and I mimicked her. David played his cello on and on.

I danced with Zuleikha, harmonized with Karolyn, clapped out simplified echoes of Geoffrey's beloved rhythms, matched the extended riffs of David's bowed and plucked strings. In that moment, as in many other moments during my life (dancing to Bobby's improvisations, talking back to the plants), the gifts of being in vibralingual communion abounded.

Those sitting in butt-flattening pews were moving as best they could while remaining seated. We were, after all, in a church sanctuary. Unlike many of my church Mommas, most of the people seated before us were trained from birth to sit down and listen up in church and (heaven forbid!) to ignore any calls from spirit to dance. But the vibe of the group was dancing. Arms were a-waving, and torsos were swaying all over the place.

I leaped off the pulpit. I leaped down and ran pulpit left into the seated ones, saying, *Stand up, dance if you feel moved to*. Dance if you feel moved to. Pew by pew, the people jumped to their feet as I passed. The people in the chapel stood up and danced in waves: oscillations, vibes, cycles, undulations, vibralingual lines.

Dancers spilled out into the aisles, and a wave of dancers circumambulated the church for so long that my back reminded me to take care and remember the recent car accident. But when everybody's arms shot up, waving high into the air for what seemed like forever, I forgot about the accident and, squatting before the wavers, chanted: Remember the ground, remember the soil, remember.

Once I saw what seemed to be a balance of Earthward and Skyward reverence, I stopped chanting. The Life in the room had a voice of its own, which Karolyn, David, Geoffrey, Zuleikha, and I had served to amplify in our sisters' and brothers' bodies. I watched the scene in wonder and rested. Finally, everyone quieted down, and we ended by acknowledging the Earth.

Afterward, Gloria Karpinski, another vibralinguist, pulled me aside and positively goosed me. Gloria has over twenty years' experience as a holistic spiritual counselor, teacher, and healer focused on understanding the dynamics of spirit, body, emotions, and mind. We had met the night before at the conference organizing meeting. Her goosing, what others might call feedback, hearticulated vibralingual skills.

You sensed the longings, the energies, and questions in the room and amplified them, she said. You gave a compelling and powerfully beautiful voice to what dwelled below the surface and called to be brought out, she said.

These are the skills of being vibralingual.

I opened the next morning's session by asking if anyone had any words to which we could lend our tongues and turn into a round. A woman called out, "babies and children," evoking an innocence in the room, an innocence matched by the simple melody and innocence of tone I then invited all gathered to sing. As we sang, I asked, "Are angels babies' children?" The question drew gasps—a sound signaling surprise, delight, an important sound in vibralingalese. Vibralingual vocabularies include tone of voice, sighs, gasps, movements of the hand to the heart or to the throat, thumpings in the stomach. Unworded or vibralingual signals express kinetic wisdom, the movement to and fro underlying all sensual perceptions. Birds do it. Bees do it. Rivers, mountains, leaves, and we do it.

Becoming vibralingual requires developing skill at sensing the unspoken, barely acknowledged, yet also present real in a moment or a community. Being vibralingual also means having the wherewithal and wisdom to discern when to translate what into which vibe. Vibralingual sensitivity requires listening as much to how something is said as to what is said. This skill develops as quickly as one is willing to stop being bamboozled by the apparent, by cultural assumptions, by the loud.

There is also a considerable quality and quantity of respect for the inarticulate, the innocent, that vibralinguists display. Vibralinguists also have the courage to sound absolutely outrageous, because what is being newly worded often does not have clearly recognized, culturally coded experiences with which to relate.

Becoming vibralingual means developing a cooperative relationship with the unknown, with mysteries. It helps to have some form of beauty in which to express what is sensed, even if only to oneself, even if silently, in dreams. To become vibralingual, caress what is sensed, respond to it as gift, revere it, develop trust in what is truthfully sensed by the inner heart, the inner ear, the inner eye and skin.

Vibralingual sensitivity attends to that which is not yet fully revealed, attends not with exploitative motivation but with liberating intent, with the intent of serving the larger, undulating, vibratory relations of Life without which none of us could live.

Do not think that being vibralingual is to be without discipline, to declare oneself licensed to blurt out whatever one perceives, to always and violently disrespect the perceptions of others. On the contrary, to become vibralingual means to become wise in perceiving and giving tongue to the restorative dance between the seen and unseen, the heard and unheard real. Such wisdom comes only with patience, practice, guidance, intention, quiet attention, devotion, humility, and prayer and in community with other vibralingual tongues and ears.

There are an infinite number of ways to practice becoming vibralingual. Try apprenticing yourself to a neighborhood cat. Activate the skills of being vibralingual by humming, by praying, by being near freely running water. Exercise your vibralingual tongues by walking more and talking less, speaking only when urged to do so by no less than Life Itself. Cultivate vibralingual mastery by practicing media celibacy one day a week, by living simply daily, by resisting addictions to fashionable and culturally mandated fun.

And remember the silence. Remember the soil. Remember the fire. Remember.

Don't hold it a-gainst me ___ I won't hold it a-gainst you ___ ba - by ___ I want you to ___ be ___ free

I wan-na be free ___ of this suf - fer-ing too ___ Don't hold it a-gainst me ___ I won't hold it a-gainst you ___

ba - by ___ I want you to ___ be ___ free ___ I wan-na be free ___ of this suf - fering ___ too ___

When must we sing? How, where, and
why must we sing when there is no mere
word alone—untouched by rhythm,
breath, intention, repetition, tone—able
to express some depth of being?

Where is the mark of water or blood
beyond which only our singing brings us
freedom, brings us home?

Excerpt from "Don't Hold It,"
written by Rachel Bagby. Copyright
1993 Breathing Music ASCAP. Used
by permission.

DEATH'S DAUGHTER

IV.

I am death's daughter

child
of the image

of cities

She
who
acknowledges
shadows

daughter
of thistime

I am
of present, of past

She
who
lives
now
what is
coming

*S*O MUCH DIED TODAY that we may live as we live in the United States: kin of the trees that gave their lives to this book, the trees transformed into hundreds of thousands of rolls of toilet paper. Treetops killed by acid rain, rivers poisoned by chemicals made from bleaching tree skin into white, white paper: all of this died.

All of this died: six thousand acres of U.S. agricultural land abandoned because of soil erosion caused by unsustainable agricultural practices. Wild American ginseng, uprooted, harvested to the brink of extinction, because of overuse in the U.S. and China, Europe and Japan. Tons of echinacea, uprooted from roadsides of the U.S. Southwest, and shipped overseas to be sold as tincture for $1.50 an ounce.

And I buy an ounce of echinacea at the U.S. market price of $9.95 to keep from succumbing to what feels like an oncoming cold, a voice-snatching discomfort closing my throat.

I am death's daughter.

I am the daughter of carrots, okra, sweet potato, kale, daughter of brown rice and quinoa, daughter of millet and oats, daughter of salmon and seaweed. These beings all gave their lives today and yesterday that I might live. These are all daughters' elders: water cycles, soil cycles, air cycles, gravity's embrace. We are their daughters, and they live and die and live again in our cells.

ELOQUENT SILENCE

J IM CROW DIED in the city of Montgomery, Alabama, the year I
was born, 1956. I am a daughter of this time. The year before,
Rosa Parks, a politically active seamstress, ignored a white man's
demand that she give him her seat in the colored section of a
Montgomery, Alabama, bus.

The white section in the front of the bus was filled. By custom,
Mrs. Rosa Parks was required to relinquish her seat in the colored
section to white patrons. This she did not do. Mrs. Parks's action
sparked a bus boycott that garnered worldwide attention and ex-
posed the prevalence of apartheid practices in the southern United
States. She later told reporters that sparking a movement of international implications was not her intent. She said her only concern was
to get home after a hard day's work.

But on that fateful December day in 1955, while I still rested in
my Momma's belly in the outwardly less discriminatory
Philadelphia, Mrs. Rosa Parks's silent refusal to give her seat to a
white man told the entire Jim Crow system of enforcing white supremacy no, no, no, no, no. Her eloquent silence was heard around
the world.

A painting of Mrs. Parks sitting in her place on the bus and looking out of the window adorns the western wall of my dining mu-

seum. The dining room is so called because it is small, the dining room table is always too cluttered with creative projects to accommodate food, and each wall is adorned with an icon of feminine power. Mrs. Rosa Parks's image rests kitty-corner to one of Ms. Katherine Dunham. Ms. Dunham shares her wall with a calligraphic rendering of poem iii of "Bringings Up and Comings 'Round"—*I am a many skinned / mixed blood . . .* The wall that faces east supports an indigo batik of three voluptuous and barebreasted Indonesian women. Kitty-corner to them is an Egyptian papyrus of three women musicians. Their custom-made frame surrounds them with the barely visible names of the nine Greek muses who preside over the arts and sciences: Calliope, Clio, Euterpe, Melpomene, Terpsicore, Erato, Polyhymnia, Urania, and Thalia.

The dining museum is often the site of singing. Its smallness, its wooden floors, its surrounding images of creative feminine power inspire poems and chanting, dances and prayers. I often stand before the image of Mrs. Rosa Parks, giving thanks, acknowledging the roaring silence of her whole-bodied refusal to collaborate with injustice. Her actions spoke loudly, louder than custom, louder than racism, louder than thought, louder than our being hypnotized by illusions, greed, and hatred projected on skin.

*She
who
acknowledges
shadows*

HE KISSED HER LIPS

MARVA IS READY for it this time, deliberately hunting it down like the half-step from lowlife that it is. She goes to the habitat where she is deeply nourished—curvaceous roads shadowed by conifer forest, perfumed by chaparral—and imagines flowering into irresistible yet impervious bait for her prey. She begins her stalking before dawn. She needs the road to herself.

The fog, a diaphanous curtain, evaporates slowly as she drives through its softly jagged edges. She drives slowly, lest she distract her carefully listening skin. As she snakes around an ancient momma redwood encircled by daughter trees, the hunted hunter streaks into her mind's eye. Her recurrent daymare—a horde of uninvited hims kissing her lips—accepts her bait. A jeering chorus of malevolent voices chants the culturally sanctioned mantra, "He Kissed Her Lips," within her inner ears.

Marva is ready. She swerves off the road as if to indulge all that usually follows—"he did this to her that, grabbed or briskly patted her eager other thing." All of it, she wants it all: the multiple comers, their pale bodies, their forcefulness, her socialized-over-centuries compulsion to comply.

Marva nabs "He Kissed Her Lips" by the i-s-s and pulls it out. She wants all of it out, out of her memory, out of each godblamed cell.

She reaches way back to evict her father's porno novels carelessly (carelessly?) left on the couch for her prepubescent inspection. "He Kissed Her Lips" stalked her from between its covers. Various scenes of various hims kissing her lips leaped through her eyes onto her brain waves at least five hundred times:

"She turned her face away from him, he gently forced it back, he kissed her lips."

"He knew he had her by the way she let their held hands brush against her thigh. He walked a few steps ahead of her then abruptly turned around. He kissed her lips."

Resisting Marva's get-back attack, "He Kissed Her Lips" kicks up memories of billboards, liquor ads, films, and an infinity of oooh baby, baby monster hits. Adds drums and a drunk father's emotional neediness. Adds classmates' fearless, entitled touch. Adds dark chocolate skin. Adds white double-bass voices. Adds anything, everything to keep her lips kissed by him.

Marva gets out of her car and stomps a bent-knee, ground-sweeping dance of self-protection. She conjures up images of her Kali-fierce sisterhood stomping and drumming right by her side.

"Out! Out! Get Out!" she screams as she whomps the air.

"Out! Out! Get Out!" her sisters echo, whomp for whomp.

Marva counters "He Kissed Her Lips" with phrases she prefers. She yells, "They kissed," and "She guided her lover's respectful, responsive hands."

A half hour passes before Marva's energy wanes. Satisfied, she swoops down to gather up the redwood needles into which she has stomped the vitality she whomped all up and down and out of "He Kissed Her Lips."

Back home, in her root cellar, Marva crosses her latest conquest off her list. She carefully places the needles into an appropriately labeled jar, seals it, and stores it on the shelf with other gallon-sized jars labeled "If You White, You Right," "You Cain't; You're a Girl," "Niggers Ain't Shit," and "You Gottu Wait Your Time."

"Nine down," she whispers, "only a couple hundred more to go." She backs out of the room. She double-bolts the door.

RESONANT RESILIENCE

MARVA IS ONE of the characters through whom I confront my shadows. She is a master of resonant resilience. Hers is among the wisest of my inner voices. When rendered speechless by a challenge and unable to decipher Life's guidance for how to proceed, I'll often lend Marva's tongue my pen. Let me tell you why.

She actively challenges the psychic residue of ongoing, socially condoned, color- and gender-coded wrongs. Her fierce commitment to freedom translates into outrageous acts that effectively redress the personal suffering born of social injustices. She enters a liberating resonance with internalized sexism and racism, first by respecting the powers of their voices and pervasive iconography, then by shouting them down and physically articulating her freedom from their influence.

She does not try to heal herself alone.

Marva's allies in maintaining her resilience include the soil, trees, air, and darkness. Her allies include dance, forgiveness, participation in a sisterhood, and bodacious practices of symbolic speech.

Marva subdues the internalized voices of ism schisms and gives them a physical form, which she then retains in jars. Her ongoing interactions with the captives stored in her root cellar free her body, mind, and spirit from health-diminishing behaviors and beliefs.

Call Marva's story a parable; call it a thrival guide in diaphanous prose.

Here is how you can practice Marva's essential resonant resilience and thrival strategies:

- Confront challenges with your entire being—physically, emotionally, mentally, sensually, energetically, imaginatively, numinously;
- Carefully consider the place in which to face difficulties. When possible, choose a place in which you love to breathe;

She goes to the habitat where she is so deeply nourished

- Become aware of your challenges' vocal dimensions. For example, have you internalized cultural mantras that reinforce voice-snatching beliefs and behaviors?

"If You White, You Right" "You Cain't; You're a Girl"
"Niggers Ain't Shit"

- Counter vocal devastation with vocal wisdom. Do this out loud.

Marva counters "He Kissed Her Lips" with phrases
she now much prefers.
She yells, "They kissed," and "She guided her lover's
respectful, responsive hands."

- Align your life with Life, and cultivate allies, a restorative community with whom you share a commitment and practices to nourish and protect one another.

Let me put Marva-as-mouthpiece aside for a moment. Let me tell you directly what Life has taught me about the importance of daughters' resonant, resilient voices.

I am forty years old as I write to you.

Momma was thirty-nine the day she moaned through life-wrenching pain that I might breathe my first breath and, eventually, sing.

As Momma would say, I have lived some. I owe my living and breathing to the music I hear and sing. I have lived to sing and study with several vocal masters, to inspire thousands of people to open their mouths and be renewed by sound, to perform in many lands, to chant with the Ganges River, to sing my poetry in the Library of Congress, to have my vocal compositions broadcast Earthwide. No brag, just vocal fact. My singing voice is not, in and of itself, a great one. But when I align my voice with Life, restorative power sings freely out of my mouth and pen.

I believe we are all natural and cultural resonating boards. Our vocal cords are stringed instruments, plucked and bowed by Life and by our caregivers long before we utter our first words. We cry out in response—resisting or amplifying the movement of air caused by others' actions, thoughts, and words.

We sing what we eat: this belief, that Life-given blessing.

I learned to receive Life's voices of resonant resilience in hard ways. I write that you may learn more easily. I write to lend my voice to the Earthwide round of daughters beginning to breathe free of the conditioning that reinforces our species' tendencies to collude with degradation—our own and that of the rest of Life. I write that we may begin to live the luminous possibilities patiently awaiting our Life-giving attention.

What I know about Life's voices of resonant resilience I learned in hard ways. Fifteen years ago I was homeless, sleeping on the cold, stone floors of women's restrooms in the San Francisco airport. Black cleaning ladies told me that these restrooms were safe. I am alive to write these words, and you receive my voice, because women whom many look down upon used their voices to protect mine.

This bears repeating: Black cleaning ladies told me in which public restrooms it would be safe for me to sleep. Then they saw to it that nobody bothered me. Somebody momma-ed those Black cleaning ladies in such a way that they grew up to momma me, a stranger's daughter with bare feet, sleeping in airport restrooms. Those cleaning ladies' voices carried on a vocal wisdom tradition that has kept daughters alive since time before time: Make safe places for one another. Tell one another where the safe places are.

"Daughter, it is safe here," their voices whispered. *"Daughter, where yo' shoes?"* they asked. *"Baby, I can't help you much, but here's a dollar. Go get yourself some food."*

Fifteen years ago, I was homeless. I will not reveal many details about how I landed in deprivation's lap. Know that something inside of me, something older and wiser than any "I" with whom to identify, survived being raped, an experience shared by an estimated one in three women in the United States.

It happened in water, water newly warmed from the womb of the brown, brown earth, brown as my skin. A man, elfin in face and in stature, offered to float me on the warm water. Innocence said yes. Full the moon. Warm the pool filled with water heated deep within Earthma's belly. Hot at the source yet cooled by the cool spring equinox air, this clear liquid earth blood, waters reflecting dark, dark sky, bright stars, and moon. So inviting, this offer from a man who could be Pan's kin.

It happened in the indigo waters of an open-air womb. Yes, I said, yes you may float me.

Slowly, head first, then shoulder, back, butt, thighs, calves, feet, I released myself to the waters, completely supported by an amniotic fluid, a support ever so lightly augmented by my escort's forearms lightly, lightly touching the nape of my neck, the small of my back. From these points of contact he slowly swept me back and forth in a figure eight before him.

I'd witnessed many other members of the spiritual community
that called the hot springs home doing the same in the warm pool
under cover of both daylight and starlight, women with women with
children with men with men. The night was that of a holy day:
spring equinox, equal day and night. I trusted Life even though I
was alone with a stranger. I trusted this holy moment. I trusted the
stories and professed values of the spiritual community to which he
belonged. I trusted this seemingly harmless human relative of Pan.

Yes, I said, innocently, yes, you may float me.

Feeling his penis stiffen in stark contrast to the waters' rippling, I
turn and face him, feel my eyes widen with surprise, then tighten with
clear intention. I tell him clearly, I am not interested in sex. He reas-
sures me, says it is not possible to penetrate me in warm water. As he
tells me this and I believe him, I feel relaxation return to my eyes. My
body surrenders again to full relaxation in Earthma's warm waters.

Sweet moment of moon gazing. Sweet the night air filled with
steam and stars shining. Sweet womb return until my escort
abruptly whips me around, rams me down on him, and comes.

daughter
of thistime

I am
of present, of past

Goddess, he called me before his supreme violation. Goddess, he
said when he lied. He rammed himself in, in, with lies. He violated
innocence. Out, out of the water I half ran, half swam in silence.

I was in shock, naked, steaming, drying myself off in the coed
dressing room when he walked in. Gentle, I told myself, it was a

gentle taking as takings go. Perhaps he misunderstood me, I told myself, when I told him how he looked like an elf and was beautiful. Innocent, my telling him so. Perhaps all the internal voices saying I deserved to be taken for being so stupid, so trusting, were right. I dressed in silence and shock.

It is said that one in three daughters in the United States is sexually taken without consent.

He said that what happened was meant to be, that we were somehow meant to be together. I felt the depth of his hunger, his loneliness. For him I felt pity. And for myself, beyond the shock, I could not feel. He still looked like one of Pan's kin. Before the taking I believed him to be a trustworthy son of the Earth, but he took a woman's body, this woman's body he took in warm water. I said nothing. I walked away.

Out into the witnessing night air I walked, silently talking to Life. Life, if this is what I can expect of my species, then why should I keep being you in this form? I asked.

And Life answered in multiple images, as if I was suddenly sitting in a theater with multiple screens. I saw rivers strewn with garbage and bubbling with chemicals, yet running, running, juxtaposed with spring singing infinite fields of lupine into being. I saw the ground in what I later came to identify as the Four Corners region of Hopi and Dine territory in the American Southwest being ripped into by giant machines mining something that killed all around. And I saw this juxtaposed with visions of fountainheads, waters, clear, laughing, free.

I saw Life's many deaths and lives and endings and beginnings and takings and healings in other-than-human form. These visions and what I heard in the music that accompanied them told me that I, too, with the proper care, would be restored.

Know that after being raped, something inside felt possessed by a chanting rape archetype (lay yo' body down, chile, lay yo' body down). Know that after being raped, truth and safety meant next to nothing and no relationships were to be trusted. Body split from mind. Mind tore away from emotion. Spirit? What was spirit?

Know that before being raped, I felt deeply betrayed by my kin's responses to the dictates of sexism and racism. I felt so deeply betrayed and confused by my own internalized ism schisms that I refused my Momma's pleas to come back to her house to begin my life again.

Know that ism schisms drove me mad. Know that I deeply, deeply hated the skin and the gender I lived in.

I WANTED TO BE WHITE. I WANTED TO BE LOVED BY THE ONES WHO WERE ALWAYS RIGHT. I WANTED TO LIVE IN A QUIET NEIGHBOR-HOOD AND EAT FANCY FOOD AND DRESS UP AND RIDE REAL HORSES AND NOT WORRY, NOT FUSS AND FIGHT ABOUT MONEY. I WANTED TO BE LOVED, AND TO BE LOVED LOOKED, ON TELEVISION, LIKE WHAT WHITE BOYS DID TO WHITE GIRLS. AND THE WHITE GIRLS SMILED AND LAID DOWN THEIR BODIES LIKE THEY LIKED IT. I WANTED TO LAY DOWN MY BODY AND LIKE IT RIGHT.

But each time I laid my body down, I hated it.

Before I took to sleeping in the San Francisco airport I was easy prey for affection-starved white men. "If You White, You Right." If a white male acquaintance liked me, I was somebody; right? Though homeless, I was still a woman if a white man wanted me, right? If he had a key to a room in which I could stay warm for the evening, I would not mind much, would I, if the price of warmth and food was a kiss? "He Kissed Her Lips." There wasn't much harm in the press of lip against reluctant lip, absent both passion and violent animosity, right?

Know that Black daughters' voices, resonant with Life, resilient in cultures that frequently tell us we are nothing, snatched me back from extreme deprivation, to this now, this privilege of speaking to you from this page.

Listen.

Only Life knows why I finally heeded the voice of wisdom, first heard on Mom Mountain, a voice insisting that I return to my Momma's house to ask for the stories of the women in her family, and learn—

I am a farmer's daughter

daughter
of daughter
of daughter

of women
who
knew
what to plant
during which growing moon

A Black classmate from Stanford Law School took me in when I told her I was homeless and needed a place to stay while I earned plane fare home. Her spare room was a safe and quiet place in which something deep inside of me started healing. *Make safe places for one another. Tell one another where the safe places are.*

Momma begged me to let her send me money to return to Philadelphia. But Momma's money couldn't buy what I needed. I needed to relearn how to make my own way in the world. I worked two jobs to earn money quickly. I was a Kelly girl typing and filing insurance reports by day and a singing waitress fending off drunks by night. My return to Momma was hastened by the terrifying night when my night boss held me captive until well past dawn and confessed his mercenary past in Africa, multiple black-faced fantasies and slights, and the habit of violently pursuing his desires. Later that morning, after the siege, I quit both jobs, packed my few belongings in double-bagged paper bags, and caught a Greyhound bus from California to Philadelphia, to my Momma's home.

Days later, Momma met me at the bus station. We rode a cab in silence to her house. Upstairs on the black vinyl sofa bed in what had been my childhood room, I begged Momma to break a legacy of holding the women's stories safe behind closed lips. I told her my life depended on hearing the stories of her daughterhood, and her Momma's daughterhood, and her Momma's daughterhood, too.

I needed to know what Momma learned as a girl. I needed to know about the roots of her belief systems to understand how, in my life, those beliefs had become poisons. I wanted to know what she knew of the wild and the trees. I needed the voices of the wombed ones in my Mommaline.

Theirs was a vocal wisdom—wisdom that they were too busy making ends meet to write. I could not live without knowing and giving voice to how they had lived. Their stories were my breath and my birthright. They restoried my soul.

Remember our ancestral assignment. It bears repeating at least as many times as the myriad instructions daughters receive to lay our bodies down before untrustworthy sons:

The women in your families have stories they may never be able to tell you in words, yet you'll live them. Listen for their unsaids in all the ways they respond to your body: passion, envy, anxiety, approval, critique. Hidden in their eagerness to raise you up straitjacket proper, hidden in the ways they let you fall, are unsaids they try to rename with your name.

Find them. Find their unsaid, unsung stories, or those stories will eat you alive.

How are we hidden from ourselves?

There in your body's health or discomfort—women's stories.
There in your hidden questions—many stories waiting to be sung.
There in your female relatives' closed lips and unspeaking eyes lie
what you may sometimes feel you're dying of—

—Phantoms of untold daughters' stories. Love them. Love these
longing-to-be-heard unsaids. Love them into being sung freely, and
then listen to the soundings of your life.

MANHOLES

M Y FATHER IS A SEXIST. He reads this and corrects me.
"I'm a chauvinist," he says.
I love my Daddy.
He is not only a sexist/chauvinist. He is also handsome. Every
holiday card he gives me reflects his understanding of my values and
his love of me. Daddy is frequently kind. He can be generous of ear,
especially when I clearly ask him to listen. His quick wit and mind
are now the chef's knife, now the sharpening stone. He is a comedic
genius. From a child, as Momma would say, he has been a master
storyteller, master of cuttin' the fool.

I do not love him because he is a sexist. I do not love his self-
defined, chauvinistic self, the self that believes in male dominance,
male superiority. Even as he does laundry, washes dishes and cooks
his dinner to give Momma a rest, the sexist part of my Daddy says
he believes that washing dishes and cooking are women's work. He
was raised that way. The last time we talked about it, Daddy said
that in his father's family . . .

I interrupted. I asked if he meant his father's brothers and sisters,
and he said no. He said he meant *his* brothers and sisters, and I said,
Oh, you mean in your Momma's and Daddy's family . . .

Daddy talks about his father's family just like I talk about
Momma's house, even though he lives there. The house is in her

name. I grew up thinking she paid for it. Daddy says he helped finance our home. Who rules? Who knows. We stayed in that house because of Momma. Momma's mouth and money and prayers kept the family alive and together during the first eleven years of my life when much of Daddy's cash financed his addictions to expensive, illicit substances.

I no longer hold his old addictions against him. For years I did. The news of his addictions came at a time when I was battling my own: to the approval of white men and to the marijuana one white man in particular made so readily available. Even now I still marvel at the destructive power of illusions engendered by ingesting such a small weed, a lightweight drug by street standards. Under the influence of this poison in my cells I ripped my life apart, for only delusions of white supremacy knows what.

Let's call the white man in question Tom. He was my wild time. He was my ticket to the woods. He was the kindly looking ghost captain to my Mrs. Mueller from a sitcom I loved to watch during childhood. He whisked me out of the staid and boring hell of Stanford Law School for a time. He took me to the ancient redwoods. He said he liked me because Black women are strong, and I didn't know to hear what he said as racism.

He was white. White was right.

Daddy's drug-influenced behavior made it clear that appearance and reality were simply words and that to find a man who truly cherished me, predictably, was more than I could hope for. Fighting was a norm in relations between the women and the men in the neighborhood of my youth. Fighting and shucking and jiving and taking all sorts of crap from a man and calling it love. The television sitcoms promised that, at least with white men, there would be some peace.

And there was. There were hours to myself to create. This was a longed-for peace, though so often short-lived. And the inner voice that said Tom was evil as he stood by my car window and cursed me —that voice just had to be wrong. Tom was white. White was right.

Moving away wasn't an option. So what if my Tommy was mean now and then? So was Daddy. When Tom told me I could do nothing to stop his meanness, I believed him. As a child, I trembled with rage as Daddy told me the same thing. It felt oh, so familiar when Tom belittled me whenever I tried to create something else between us, tried to apply my brain to the problem we were facing, tried to say there was another way.

So did Daddy.

I remembered Daddy's and Momma's regular, frightening arguments. I remembered my Daddy using his mouth as a weapon and raising his voice and calling Momma stupid to belittle her. I remembered Daddy storming around and slamming doors and staying away for hours and coming home apologetic and all smelly. Like mother, like daughter. Like father, like old white boyfriend.

I called Daddy as I struggled with a legacy of his addiction to drugs and my own to the prevalent fantasies of white men as gods, no matter how meanly they act. I called and told him I was smoking marijuana daily. My call was a hidden cry for help. In response, Daddy told me what I struggled with wasn't nothing.

He told me that he sported a sixty-thousand-dollars-a-year heroin habit, give or take a zero, when we were growing up. Oh, what a big difference nothing can make. He bragged of sharing suppliers with Coltrane and Lady Day. He told me the supplier's name—the father of one of my girlfriends. Daddy used to take me to see the little girl of the house. Were we decoys? Did Daddy tell Momma he was taking me to play with my friend?

How did you support your habit? I asked Daddy, shocked. Petty larceny, he replied. When I heard his answer, something inside decided that I must be really worthless if what he said was true. I knew how hard Momma worked to make ends meet. If I heard them argue once over money I heard them argue ten thousand times, give or take a zero. How could he manage to finance a heroin habit when sometimes all Momma could afford to feed us was Wonder Bread and Aunt Jemima's corn syrup?

I love my Daddy. I still don't understand how my feeling of compassion toward him lives side by side so deeply with a wariness toward him. I still don't trust that he won't Jekyll-and-Hyde out on me, even though he hasn't taken drugs or stormed or slammed or come home smelling like a bar for nearly thirty years.

But I still say he is a sexist.

He is not only that.

These days he helps Momma in her community work. He says he owes Momma the cooperation of his elder years partly because of the time he spent cuttin' the fool in the streets.

I love my Daddy. The part of me that was well trained by him often claims my tongue with a shucking and a quality of loving that several middle-class Black men have told me feels like hatred; it's so rough. Cultures clash. This is part of what I learned meant love: loud talk, toasting, and bad mouthing. Wolfing is how we bond. I am my Daddy's daughter.

He picked up the phone when I called home. I called for help and did not know to ask for Momma. I called high and was shocked. Daddy mocked my little habit. Told me how big his was. Didn't warn me away. Didn't tell me to come home. Didn't know how to hold me back from marijuana, the younger demon relative of the demons that once almost killed him.

Life, he tells me. Life, the reason for Nelson's preferential treatment. Unreasonable, I'm being unreasonable, Daddy says, when I fight for his acknowledgment of my perceptions; perceptions he tries to deny. I am near forty when I confront his sexism head-on. I am in my New Hampshire home in the kitchen, up against the counter. Daddy is in Philadelphia, on the kitchen phone. The cord of my phone twists behind my neck as I feel like I'm being punched in the stomach, again and again, up against the counter, on my tippy-toes.

"You listen to me!" I yell at him. "You listen to me first, and then I'll listen to you. You did show Nelson favoritism, I didn't imagine this. It was not just Momma all over me about my clothes and my hair, but you are a sexist and showed Nelson favor. This happened," I say.

"Well, yes, I don't deny that it happened," Daddy finally admits, "but it wasn't wrong. What you expect me to do, apologize? That I will not do."

His refusal takes my breath away. Not until he says what he says do I recognize the depths at which I wanted the gift of his apology. How I longed to hear him say, "I'm sorry my actions hurt you, baby. Please forgive me."

Never has the distance between desire and expectation felt so impossibly wide.

I cannot, do not, in that moment speak the obvious analogy: You are telling me that your feeling about men being superior to women is Life. Well, then, when a white boy gets in your face about being superior to your black behind, is that Life, too, Daddy dearest? Is that Life?

Thank Life such lies are not all the life there is. Tonight, watching *Deep Space 9,* I watch a warrior people addicted to a substance called "white" walk knowingly into a canyon from which there is

195   MANHOLES

no escape. The Starfleet captain, a Black man, walks out to offer them an alternative. He tells them that they were betrayed. He says their leader set the trap so that they would be killed.

The addicted being says he will follow his orders. Surrender, the captain urges. Surrender, and we'll sedate your men until we get more white, and you'll be free.

Our leader didn't give us the option of surrendering, the warrior says.

But, man, the captain says, your leader does not deserve your loyalty.

He cannot earn my loyalty, the warrior says. Doesn't have to. He has it, has had it since the day that I was conceived.

The captain says, you will give your life to maintain the order of things?

The warrior, a slave to substances and beliefs, says, my life was never my own. It has always belonged to the Founders. He goes back to the other warriors and says, It is glory to the Founders to die fighting for them.

Then they do.

The warrior is a slave. So, too, was I enslaved by the beliefs we lived in our house and those surrounding us, beliefs saturating the very air we breathed.

My Daddy watches murder and violence on television because that is what is on, he says, and they only get three channels, he says, and the air in the house is filled, to this day, with the commotion and conflict that some call entertainment.

Fallacies and televised fantasies. Enslaving ideals taken as the order of things. *Oh, Life, have mercy.*

After *Deep Space 9* is over I think of Daddy, and of being conditioned to be like the warriors, addicted to white, white, white. Following the programs saturating our culture, twisted cultural programs reinforced by televised fantasies, I walked into many valleys of evil. I entered relationships with abusive white men and thought I was privileged to be with them because, of course, they are white and right.

Martin, my husband and partner of almost fifteen years, asks me what is on my mind as I stare out into the room after watching *Deep Space 9*. I tell him: If my father were white and told me he believed in racism, believed in white supremacy, his beliefs could not cut me more deeply than does my Daddy's sexism. I tell my husband this because he is a Black man who studies race, and since he is a man I don't expect him to fully understand how Daddy's conditioning set me up for rape. The pain of familial sexism is perhaps more accessible to Martin through the lens of race, since he is conscious of having suffered some of the persistent injustices of racism and has studied more of them.

I have not yet, as of this writing, talked with Daddy about the shared falsehoods of racism and sexism and about both being power-based beliefs that can turn family against one another.

My Daddy is a sexist. Time after time, the conflicted love I feel for Daddy comes to heart and mind as I listen to the stories August Wilson tells at the opening of each playwriting class.

Wilson, two-time Pulitzer Prize–winning playwright, tells us to call him our guide. I love much about him, not the least of which is how he opens every class with a story about his life in Pittsburgh, a story that gives me a Pittsburgh I never knew while there as a college student.

His class is part of his quarter-long residency as a Montgomery Fellow at Dartmouth. To apply for a coveted seat in the class, we were asked to write a two-page response to this question: Why did you learn to read?

Here is my response:

Why the Rachels Bagby Learned to Read

Who you asking?

I learned to read because my Momma, Rachel Edna Samiella Rebecca Jones Bagby, learned to read before me, as did her Momma before her. My Mommaline is only three generations of readers deep in this country. Our eldest known ancestor, my Great-Grandmomma Liz, was neither a Rachel nor a reader. But Elizabeth Minerva Simianne Texas Jennings was a strong dreamer, and her dreams for her family usually came true.

In Civil War–torn Cope, South Carolina, she dreamed herself free and married, with over a hundred acres, horses, cows, pigs, fowl, and many mules to her name, and her dream came true. She dreamed up seven children all reading themselves through college. She dreamed whatever trouble was coming—storms, the KKK—before it came and dreamed how to keep it from troubling her. She died a dream kinda dying when at one hundred and four years of age she swept her kitchen floor, sat down, and peacefully breathed her last breath.

Did you *why* your first breathing?

Ever since I can remember, reading has been like breathing in my family. Among my kith and kin, reading runs right alongside loud talking and lip music, wolfing, and jumping bad. So I asked my Momma what she remembered about why our reading began. Expected her usual "*good* gracious, what kinda question is that" response. I frequently ask Momma "why did you learn how to read" kinda questions:

Why did you move to Philly and stay if the houses were smaller than your horses' stables, and the water nasty and the people runnin' all around like wild animules?

Why do your dining room walls hold seven different pictures of Jesus with white skin, blond hair, and blue eyes if you say that the God you worship ain't white, yet, every day, you pray to Jesus?

Lord have mercy, I *had* to learn how to read, Momma said, 'cause old folks wouldn't tell you much. A lot of times they wouldn't tell you things, and you'd pick up papers and wonder, "What in the devil is this?"

I got a better understanding when I learned how to read, better than talking to people. Out on the farm, you didn't have no whole lot of people to talk to. I was the oldest child in my family by some years. My cousins were much older, but I didn't like them 'cause of all their drinking and carrying on. So I didn't believe nothing they say anyway.

A reading world and other ways of acting opened up to you when you learned how to read. We been hampered in a lot of ways, but not being able to read wasn't going to be one of them for me or mine, so help me Jesus, Momma said.

What's *why* got to do with it?

I read in self-defense. Read myself out of roach infestations and Momma and Daddy going at it for the umpteenth time. When reading about Dick and Jane and Spot bored me into belligerence and the slow/bad class, I got good books out of the library to prove I was smart. Momma and I read all sorts of papers that helped me test into the accelerated class. I used what I read to sass Daddy's loud-talking and wolfing friends.

As I learned how to read, I learned how to write and to ask my Momma lifetimes of questions and record her answers so that what she learned from Great-Grandmomma Liz would not be lost.

I learned to read 'cause Great Grandmomma Liz dreamed me reading. And her dream came true.

I learn much in August Wilson's playwriting class, not the least of which is how and why I can love my Daddy, name his sexism as such, and still respect myself.

For our next-to-last assignment, August Wilson tells us to make one up, one that he would assign. Here is mine:

Assignment #15—Submit a two-page answer to the following question: How has your participation in class thus far enriched your spiritual resources?

Wilson liked the assignment so much that he made it the final one for the class. Here is what I wrote in response and read aloud at our final session in the Montgomery House:

I no longer run from words that feel like guns pointed at an unnamed daughter's vagina, guns holstered in the silk intention of teaching us our craft.

We learn the craft of dramatic tension through a story of a courageous yet dead, stolen daughter. There is more to the story, of course. But here I have only two pages. *Select. Arrange. Discard.*

The story in question taught me how the teller set us up. The polyrhythms of meeting and conquering and being conquered did not fall on deaf ears. The story was filled with dead and bleeding men. I know that death and blood and violence and the pheromone-inspired follies of my brothers are legion, legendary, and a very vocal kind of real.

I do not write this lightly. I write this with the memory of looking down the barrel of a real-live gun. I stood behind the counter of the Burger King, terrified, pressed against the cash register. The man on the other end of the weapon told me to open the drawer. I obeyed him.

In walked my Daddy to pick me up from work. He stood shoulder-to-shoulder next to the armed young man, a man close in age and milk chocolate complexion to my brother. My dad stood next to him like they were friends. I wondered.

Daddy said, "Let's go," and I looked at him like he was crazy. He wasn't so old or blind that he couldn't see the gun, pointing at my heart, shiny as it was. He repeated himself, calmly, "I said, let's go, baby," and motioned with his head toward the door.

All that was real in that moment was the gun, my thumping heart, and Daddy's chocolate-bass directions. Perhaps my life was too short to flash before me. I was not yet fifteen. Perhaps the death flash didn't come because my Daddy *really* knew something, knew from the sense knocked into his life by the streets that the man next to him only wanted the money. Perhaps my Daddy and the gunman were in cahoots and we'd split the take later; split it three ways.

"Let's go, baby," Daddy said again. "Leave the drawer open and come on." The third time his voice worked like a charm, unglued my feet from the spot on the floor where time had no meaning and movement was impossible because space did not exist. Trembling, I followed directions. I walked out of that Burger King silently beside my savior, exhoodlum Daddy. No daughter ever had a finer escort to a car. We didn't talk about anything as he drove me home. We never told my Momma what happened; what took us so long.

And only this week did I ask Daddy if he knew the gunman standing before us. He did not. I asked if he was afraid. "Wasn't no time to be afraid," Daddy answered softly, matter-of-fact.

It is a matter of fact that every woman alive is somebody's daughter. It is a fact that one of every three daughters in the United States will suffer sexual abuse, some at the hands of their own kin. It is true that our species lets blood, for the damnedest reasons.

And even though I am battle weary of learning craft through blood-stained stories, I am learning to face the truths of this way of learning and living on the spectrum of the possible without being drained.

I am more courageous. I am less ashamed. These are enlarged spiritual resources.

My journals are filled with my struggles over the places on Life's wheel where the men who love daughters also see womankind as objects to be owned, to kill or be killed for. In another world, this place is occupied by Great-Granddad, the white man, telling his cherrywood-brown son that he loves him deeply while simultaneously embodying the values of white supremacy.

I am learning to keep breathing and imagining power-filled daughters in the face of (August Wilson) a cherished guide declaring imagined daughters and their bodacious powers implausible. Simultaneously, his teachings inspire me to develop creatively without the bamboozlements of white supremacy telling me what colored brilliance can or cannot be so. For this, I am profoundly grateful. And I do not yet know the depth of spiritual enlargement being seeded in me by these gifts.

What I do know is that I see my Daddy differently. I treasure his stories now, again, seventeen years after my discovery of feminism. Seventeen years after my Daddy became a hated emissary of daughter-stealing, daughter-stabbing, daughter-strangling patriarchy, I am learning to forgive him his sins of ism schisms.

As I forgive my own, many more times than seventy times seven.

The guide's stories release me from judgments of the junkies who helped keep me alive without catching me as they were caught. In light of this learning, "do as I say and not as I do" becomes a *blessed* hypocrisy.

In the process of researching the oh-so-male cigar culture for our final project, I find this creation story on the Web:

Huron Indian myth has it that in ancient times, when the land was barren and the people were starving, the Great Spirit sent forth a woman to save humanity. As she traveled over the world, everywhere her right hand touched the soil, there grew potatoes. *(I bet some of them were sweet!)* And everywhere her left hand touched the soil, there grew corn. And when the world was rich and fertile, she sat down and rested. When she arose, there grew tobacco. . . .

I am less judgmental. I am more at home. Nothing in my world is the same.

Seventy Times Seven

I.

I swallow stones of my sorrows
But unlike birds' voices
well-fed by pebbly feasts
My voice rankles in rock beds

Try singing with stones in your mouth. If singing is too hard because you choke on the stones each time you open wide enough to release a tone, try talking. If stones in the mouth prevent talking, try pebbles instead: one pebble each for all you have yet to forgive.

II.

Forgive. Forgive. Forgive.

Why forgive? Forgive because the unforgiven stifles breathing's wisdom.

When to forgive? Forgive when you are ready to be forgiven. Forgive when you can fully receive and release the grief, the anger, the difficult feelings that often accompany soul-deep healing.

Whom to forgive? Forgive the Life-denying daughter you were raised to be.

What to forgive? Forgive all self-denigration you embrace to survive.

How to forgive? Often. Truthfully.

III.

True forgiveness is not condescending.

Forgiveness does not require you to surrender to the cruelty of thrown or spoken stones.

True forgiveness does not make you dumb.

Forgiveness is not an invitation to self-destruct by trying to embody the dictum that daughters be *pinked out / . . . tasty / and everything nice.*

True forgiveness is not self-hatred masquerading as nobility.

True forgiveness does not require telling or living bold-faced or subtle emotional lies.

IV.

Find stones the size of whatever parts of your body register pain whenever you confront systematic injustices. If your breathing suffers in response to suffering, gather enough stones to fill in a silhouette of your body outlined on the floor by a friend.

Lie down next to your stone parts, and have your friend cover your flesh with collected hardness.

Try breathing deeply. Try speaking persuasively. Try singing out loud.

V.

As you begin to forgive, it helps to keep in mind a list of at least ten truly lovable nonthings about yourself. It helps to write this love list down.

It helps to remember ten moments in which you offered others effortless kindness. Please, receive your effortless kindness.

It helps to tell yourself, out loud, of your good-heartedness.

These helpers may help you feel worthy of being blessed by forgiveness.

VI.

You need not pursue what is ready to be forgiven. Listen. Invite your luminous voice into full-bodied being, and all that replies no to your yeses will arise. Listen. Form, then repeat, your intentions to free yourself of resentments' weapons and of regrets' breath-snatching shame.

Listen.

Receive and release all suffering memories, all unhealing pain. Listen. Receive and release the stones of your sorrows again and again, without reservation.

Listen.

VII.

Enough water over rocks makes music. Try watering the stones of your sorrows into singing.

Try writing seventy declarations of self-forgiveness for seven consecutive days.

I forgive myself for habitually pushing my body into sickness. I forgive myself for disrespecting daughters' gifts for so long. I forgive myself for committing bold and subtle prostitutions in the name of survival. I forgive myself for swallowing culturally sanctioned sorrows' stones.

I forgive.

I am
of present, of past

MAHAPAJAPATI
BUDDHA'S FIRST DAUGHTER

HE DENIED ME THRICE. He denied me, the woman who suckled and raised him after my sister, his mother, died. He denied his own teachings when he told me no, women could not join his order of students, could not lead the homeless life that he said would guarantee us absolute freedom in our lifetimes.

Please, I asked, please, I asked, please.

No, no, no, he said, the final time telling me not to ask him again.

I obeyed him, of course, and didn't ask a fourth time. He was the shining one. But I knew that he shone with a light not of his own making. What he realized was deathless, he said so. What he realized had never been born, he said so himself. I knew of his birth, witnessed his boyhood. I knew him before his body became so filled with light that many awakened by the mere sight of him.

Some who awakened were women.

Yet he told me not to ask him again to accept women as nuns in his sangha, his holy order, so I didn't.

Instead of asking, I acted.

I convinced several Sakyan women, women of Buddha's tribe, to join me in cutting off our hair, putting on the saffron-colored robes of the already ordained, and walking, barefooted, one hundred fifty miles to the Great Grove. There I stood, weeping, outside of

Buddha's Kutagara Hall. Widowed women, women deserted by the men who aspired to spiritual freedom, women longing to avoid the consort, wife, mother, widow daze, come, I said.

Come, they did.

We were enlightenment's daughters, obeying our luminous yearning rather than one bright man's turning us away.

I stood, covered with dust, feet swollen, weeping, outside the hall. The Venerable Ananda, one of the Buddha's disciples, saw me, took pity upon us, and asked the Buddha to give us permission to be as we were. Three times, the Blessed One said, "Enough, Ananda. Don't set your heart on women being allowed to do this."

Ananda took another tack. He asked if women as well as men were able to realize perfection. Buddha answered yes. Well, then, Ananda said, if women were *able* to realize perfection, and since Mahapajapati had been of such service as aunt, nurse, foster mother, and nursemaid (for liberation's sake!), then it would be good to give women permission to do what they had already done: shave off their hair, leave their homes, and put on the robes of ordination.

Buddha said yes, if we agreed to live by the Eight Special Rules, which simply said no matter how special we were, the youngest monk was more so and had to be respected as an elder.

I protested, of course, and asked to change the most blatantly sexist rule, that the most senior nun bow before even the most novice monk. You can guess what happened.

Still, I accepted the terms that relegated us to secondary status in the enlightened order. We were at least in the order and somewhat protected to devote each breath to our passion for freedom. You had to have been there to know the miracle of getting the qualified yes and the training that we did.

Some call my actions skillful means. Some call me a schemer. Women who realize our dreams of living lives devoted to the middle way's promise of freedom are called, to this day, Buddha's Daughters.

I did the best I could for my life and times and for daughters coming after me. Do you, dear daughters, with all the freedoms you have, do the same?

*She
who
lives
now
what is
coming*

DIVINE DAUGHTER SISTERS: AN INITIATION

I don't know how long it will take until our entire species recognizes daughters' divinity. Nor do I know if there was ever a time or place when our kind felt ourselves to be in intimately blessed relations with all of Life.

Without the guidance of elders, and with our instincts impaired, how do we face what could be a fatal unknowing of how to come 'round to more restorative ways of living?

What are your families' women's ways in the dark? How do the elder daughters among you retrieve forgotten wisdom, learn new wisdom ways? How do we collectively reclaim and reinvent wisdom that has been snatched away?

These are the questions with which I respond to daughters' questions, "How long will it take for all daughters to realize our holiness?" and "To what historical clues can we turn?"

What our Mommas embrace as wisdom often feels like daggers held to our breasts. Their personal histories give us a wisdom that is often rooted in arrogant ignorance of our biological, emotional, spiritual, creative, and intellectual lives. Rather than stating our experience and memory as pronouncements upon others, as Momma did with me while I was miscarrying a much-wanted baby, we elder daughters must practice passing on our stories in ways that call the mysteries contained therein by their proper names: mysteries.

Let me explain. In the middle of my recent miscarriage, my midwife told me to call my Momma and ask her about her pregnancy experiences. The part of Momma's story that seemed particularly relevant involved her bleeding throughout all her pregnancies.

When Momma first told me about her bleeding pregnancies, I didn't know then to ask her about fibroids. I didn't know how important an early knowledge of fibroids might be during my childbearing years. On the fateful day that I called her, I stayed in bed trying to quiet the contractions that felt more powerful than any menstrual cramping I'd ever had.

The entire family had been ecstatic over the news of my pregnancy. The pressure to procreate had been on for some time from my father and husband, echoed in my Momma's frequent reminders about my husband's desire for children.

"What about my desire for a healthy community to help me balance my other expressions of creativity with the demands involved in parenting children?" I had asked. I wondered about the other creations I felt compelled to serve and how they would coexist with a little, breathing, two-legged one brought out of my body.

I never felt the desire for a baby as strongly as I did when threatened with the loss of the one I'd newly learned was growing inside. At my midwife's prompting, I called Momma for more information about the quality and quantity of her bleeding while pregnant.

"Momma," I said quietly, "my midwife told me to call you to find out more about how it was for you to be pregnant and bleed."

I write this to you through tears, daughter sisters. Please learn as much as you can about your life in your mothers' bellies long before you even consider carrying a new life in your own. To lose a life once begun inside can sometimes leave a feeling of failure deep within you, a feeling oh, so difficult to dwell beside.

Being on the verge of losing a new life is not the best time to ask your Momma about her difficulties carrying you. Who knows what she suffered then, or what your suffering now will evoke? Who knows what unresolved feelings will roar out of her mouth to add another disquieting influence to your already vulnerable breathing? The powers of emotional and physiological bonds within ourselves and between daughters and Mommas are barely understood. From my own painful experience, some of which still feels stuck in my throat as I write you, I tell you that the midst of a troubled pregnancy is not the best time to explore those powers.

I must also acknowledge that we don't always get to choose the timing of our most challenging Life lessons. I certainly did not consciously choose to wait until being in the midst of a threatened miscarriage before asking my Momma for details about her bleeding pregnancies.

But there we were. In a quiet, slow voice I asked her. She never mentioned the word *fibroid* in her answer. When she finished answering, she asked me why I asked.

"Because I am bleeding, and my midwife said knowing more about your experience might help me with mine," I responded.

"You musta done something wrong," Momma said. "You know how you are. Even the way you stride . . ."

I cut her off before she could finish her sentence. I thanked her for her information and told her I'd call her in two days. In three short sentences, Momma had passed on to me a devastating ignorance, and I felt blamed, felt flawed and inadequate, and had to hang up to cry. In that moment, I noticed more clearly than ever before how deeply what Momma says affects me.

The miscarriage books say feelings of inadequacy will come and go. And, daughter sisters, we do not know why most miscarriages happen, only that they frequently happen, often without our knowledge.

Miscarriages are a painful place of womanly unknowing. Momma passed on to me what the doctors passed on to her when she had pregnancy troubles: she musta done something wrong. If a woman can't hold a baby, she musta done something wrong; it's her fault rather than another expression of life's and death's many mysteries or an incidence of natural selection or some possible problem with the baby's chromosomes.

Momma said she could not go as deep as chromosomes because she didn't know about them. She could only go only as far as a woman's weak, wrong body. She could go only as far with me as others had gone with her and as far as she had managed to go with herself.

In that moment of my need for comfort and for information, my Momma passed me painful, poisonous blame. We have since talked about that moment, learned much from it, healed. Thank Life for the depths of compassion and forgiveness Momma and I have learned to practice with each other over the years.

Having danced so intimately with death, I have turned to face my living with new eyes. Boop, the affectionate name my husband and I called our unborn, still grows in consciousness, bringing me into a new honesty about my relations with this body, with life, with death.

What a joy to be daughter! What a marvel to be able to give birth to other daughters and sons! Even in the midst of losing Boop, I was awestruck at how powerful our bodies are. Though framed by sorrow, the waves of movements that swept Boop out of me were accompanied by an unexpected ecstasy.

A tinge of fear regarding how you'll perceive my telling you about this experience threatens to silence my pen. I feel I should change the subject quickly or, at the very least, give you a more conventional rendition of what happened.

Learning how to stay true to Life despite such emotions is one of my deepest lessons and blessings from losing Boop. I've messed around for years in depths of self-betrayal, a consequence of Self-unknowing. In trying to emulate media images of successful white boys and thereby gain access to their social and material powers, I may have worked too hard and waited too long to do what no white boy (or any boy!) can of his own body do: carry and give birth to children.

To recognize and revere the powers of giving birth is not very popular in many of the ecological and feminist circles I still call home. But Boop's being here and so soon gone taught me that no external association is worth ignoring Life's call to participate so intimately in life.

Now, I let nothing distract me. Now, I guard my time and wrestle with *Now, Now, Now*, rather than with my fears of being rejected by the powerful *them* I think I must please in order to have company and the resources I crave for creative freedom. Now, as I lie recovering on the couch that has been my friend forever, I vow to you, daughter sisters, that I am becoming free of these silken bridles on my tongue. On this couch that shielded me as a child from the rage and glass splattering the streets following the assassination of Martin Luther King, Jr., I release intergenerational habits of self-strangulation in the name of pleasing others.

I need to tell you that giving birth to death is an initiation. It is an initiation complete with the formidable bodily stresses of giving birth to a baby. I pray you never find yourselves in my place. But if you do, be kind to your body. Treat yourself with the respect of one who has just given birth. With no baby there to remind you to slow down, no little life reflecting back your holiness, you will need to call around you others who will help you grieve and help you return to strength.

Do call them, soon and often. If you have the privilege of lying down and listening when your body says ouch!, do so. Tend to your recovery steadily and early.

I imagine there might be at least one other way for daughters to learn what we need to know about our bodies and the miraculous ability we have to bring forth other human lives. For all daughters, I wish divine daughter councils. For all, I pray there to be a circle of knowing, a circle constantly growing in wisdom through contact between younger and older daughters. I urge us all to create divine daughter circles where, rather than stating experience as prophecy, we say what we think we know. We hear what the elder daughters have learned to bear through only Life knows what and how. We learn of their still-unanswered questions, their still-healing sorrows. We learn what the younger daughters yearn to experience and understand. We learn what the younger daughters know about freedom and giving it voice.

In the face of unknowing, daughters, let us sit in circle, in council, regularly, to speak our wisdom, ask our questions, and grow. Let us sit in council to learn, to listen, to feel, to sense wisdom, deep-down wisdom, wisdom dirt deep, deeper than skin and inherited notions of sin. Let us sit in the round to round out our knowledge, to circle our yearning into our warm and open hearts. Let us sit, encircling and encircled by Life as we live and rekindle wise wonder.

Slowly

Re - ceive re - ceive _____ re - ceive _____ re - - ceive _____

How does Life sing us?

Let us live the ways.

Excerpt from "Receive," written by
Rachel Bagby. Copyright 1993
Breathing Music ASCAP.
Used by permission.

v.

I am all daughters

all someday mothers
of daughters
of sons

music
of growing things

still

darkness and colors

of theretime
in heretime

We
who
create
what is
coming

D IVINE DAUGHTER SISTERS: ALL DAUGHTERS
The space between "I am all daughters" and "all someday
mothers" is essential. Do not collapse it. Do not read too, too
quickly over all its emptiness implies.

While not all daughters will be mothers someday, all mothers are first daughters. How we are treated as daughters reflects how our mothers were daughtered and how our fathers were sonned. How we are daughtered influences how we will, if we will, mother other beings, human and non.

And how we are daughtered deeply influences how we do or do not nurture the voices of our creative impulses and the lap of Life in which they arise.

Create what is coming. Divine, daughters. Verb your very breath. Verb your she being. Divine your life's meaning echoed by Life as you live and you breathe. Divine daughters. Divine, ask for Life's guidance. Ask to be music of growing things as surely as our exhaled waste, our carbon dioxide, is welcomed by leaves, and their waste, their oxygen, fuel for our songs.

Ask for the blessings of strengthening stillness. Ask for the blessings of a clarifying quietness of mind with which to see how your nowtime is born of both heretime and theretime. See if how you now live reflects or reacts to the there of your mothers' mothers' hopes and dreams and fears. See if how you now live reflects the here of your culture's beliefs and legacies, denials and gifts.

From all this, create what is coming, daughter sisters, create. Divine and give voice to your dreams.

GIRLS ARE GREAT

I ARRIVED CHANTING, carrying flip charts and vividly colored markers: sunrise fuchsia, blue spruce blue, iris purple, sunset orange, early spring *green*green. I arrived with singing, candles, and a plan impassioned by the dream-come-true assignment of helping to bring daughters' full voices 'round to Life.

The occasion: "Girls Are Great," a day of exploration held at the Darmouth-Hitchcock Medical Center in Hanover, New Hampshire. Cosponsored by the Women's Resource Center and the Swift Water Girl Scout Council, "Girls Are Great" gathered together some one hundred daughters—younger and elder—to steep in girls' greatness.

Glory be.

Each of four groups made the rounds to four sessions: Celebrating Our Bodies and Voices; Eating Right/Body Image and the Media; Your Changing Body; and Self-Esteem. I co-led the one devoted to creative expression with a daughter who focused on movement.

Before me breathed twenty-five daughters; twelve of whom were in grades four through six. The rest of us, daughters all, were their mothers, companions, or eager guides. I called for us to give and receive our names with the quality of sound and Life we wanted to hear echoed in the voices of our companions.

Our voices are gifts we give and receive, I said. How does Life sing us? Let's explore some ways. First, I sang my name into a candle to show the power of our very breath to affect other forms of vibrant Life. Next, I said my name, *Rachel,* barely audible and invited all present to mimic what they heard. The group-whispered echo *Rachel* sounded like a cherished secret spreading—daughter to daughter—around the room. My next demonstration, leaping into the circle's center as I hurled my arms and name to the blazing blue sky outside, drew laughter and waves of bold leaps by younger and older daughters colliding with one another as we each filled the space.

Some daughters, elder and younger, responded shyly to my guidance. Others danced their names out, *loud*. I was struck by how often the shyness or outspokenness of the younger daughters mirrored that of their elder companion.

Then, I called for what comes to mind and mouth in response to the word *voice*. I recorded the offerings in a colored spiral on a flip chart and talked all the while about the powers of our voices to change and shape reality, as our voices created the colorful spiral of wisdom unfurling before us.

Moving from giving and receiving our names to speaking and singing out color-filled spiraling words to creating a chant, we articulated girls' greatness. We spoke, we defined, we recorded and were recorded. We challenged. We gathered in circle and in younger- and elder-daughter groups. We reflected and talked.

We listened. We joined together in song. We kept together in time and created good times of our own. We gave Life and one another our names and echoed them. We called and we responded.

Voice, Voice, Voice, Voice, Voice, Voice, Voice.

Ours were the voices of poetry and the voices of definition. Ours were voices of learning and authority both challenged and allowed to lead. We did our best. We made mistakes and made the most of what we had. We were brilliant and bumbling, connected and estranged. We supported, encouraged, celebrated, resisted, struck out, and followed. We sang, we danced, and we kept together in time, chanting, to the lunch line.

I ate lunch with two friends who share my passion for bringing daughters' voices to Life. We talked about boisterous daughters, ones who are in full voice and oftentimes clueless about their impact on others. We each remembered either being *the one* or teaching a daughter who was the loudmouth, the one around whom others barely breathed.

We remembered and talked about the challenges of making room for the quiet daughters while not stifling those who were more outspoken. We asked each other and ourselves how to dance the dance of equality. We strategized ways of encouraging the skill of listening rather than asking a daughter to shut up. That approach, we reasoned, would be more in tune with our desire to amplify daughters' voices.

Even so, I admitted that there were some daughters' voices I didn't particularly want to hear. I admitted having biases and preferences and tolerances and boundaries and capacities and weaknesses and developing edges and learning spots.

After lunch, as if on cue, I was faced with such an outspoken daughter. Every question I asked, she answered as though I was speaking only to her. I could tell who her significant elder was because she seemed to disappear farther and farther back into the other side of the room each time the outspoken younger daughter opened her mouth. Other elder daughters glowered at the talker and the woman who looked so much like her that she must have been her mother. They'd already been through two other sessions together. Their cutting eyes and exaggerated or held breaths told me the outspoken daughter's behavior had yet to be effectively addressed. The third time she blurted out her response to something I said, I met her behavior head-on.

"Well, now, we are all learning something here," I said to the entire group. Then, to the voiceful daughter, "There must be some way for you to participate and still let there be room for other daughters in the room to speak."

I turned back to address all the daughters gathered: slinking-back mother, glowering others, peers unable to get a word in edgewise. I said, "Here we all have the chance to learn something about hearing our own voices and listening for the voices of others."

Only at this writing, years after the Girls Are Great day, do I wonder if my partner for the creative expression sessions considered me a hypocrite as I spoke.

Planning for the day was well under way before I'd heard about it and arrived filled with ideas, energy, and a reputation for being outrageously creative. Before I arrived, my partner had the entire creative expression hour to herself. Where was there time for her to say, No, I don't want to share this time with Rachel? With hindsight, I realize that if she'd had a desire for creative autonomy, there was no graceful way to say so.

But her behavior throughout the process clearly communicated distress. We never managed to get together for the extensive collaborative meetings I hoped for. We'd set one meeting time, she'd change it. My traveling schedule restricted our options. The one time we did manage to get together, it was for much too short a time, and the depths of feelings between us were never directly acknowledged.

I never said, "You act like you have some misgivings about our working together. It seems as though you're not exactly comfortable with the idea."

My passion for bringing daughters' voices to Life put one of Life's creative daughters between a hard place and me. It took months for me to acknowledge and to ask my partner to forgive my mistakes in our collaboration. How do we make room for each other, indeed.

This is an echo: *Listen to the emotional communications that never quite make it into words. Listen to the body's languages, and*

give them our tongues. Become vibralingual. Call ourselves into
named beings in the hopes of being clearly heard. Remember: en-
couraging daughters' voices requires listening, listening, listening to
what we are saying with our tongues and with the emotional tones
of our unworded beings.

My rhythm of directing my speech back-and-forth from the outspoken daughter to the group served to knit us together again: voice
as healer, voice as needle and thread.

"There must be some way for you to stay involved while also
leaving room for other daughters to have some say," I said. "You get
to have your responses and feelings, but experiment with allowing
other daughters present to speak first.

"Let's all experiment with how to make sure everyone present has
room for their voice. Otherwise, we will miss the voices of the quiet
ones in the room, miss their ideas and creative contributions, if you
answer every question so quickly.

"And don't worry," I said. "Your voice won't be left out."

More daughters began to speak up. The outspoken daughter's
voice was still very present, but now there was breathing room. The
chant we created at the end of that group became the one I used for
the spiral dance during the closing circle.

Why, oh, why didn't anybody *tell me* about their plan to have a
photographer present in the closing circle? I was too concerned and
watchful about the mere moments we had to clear and prepare the
room to pay attention to the hunk with the camera who suddenly
appeared at the end of the day.

I was so busy waiting for the proper time to reset the room and
fending off one of my colleague's fretfulness over the difficulty of the
tight transition we needed to make to attend to the hunk. Had I
been more truly present perhaps I would have known that his presence meant serious trouble.

I was also distracted by the pain leftover from injuring my foot during one of the morning sessions. And my dear friend Debbie, the woman who would know to keep that man out of the spiral, was being ever focused on the task of preparing the room for our closing circle.

Did he ask for the assignment? Was there a rotation of photographers and his was just the luck of the draw? Was there simply no one at the local newspaper who knew any better than to assign "Girls Are Great" to this particular man? The day was about girls and their greatness, giving voices to girls' dreams, eschewing cultural signals regarding body images, and you send a well-built young man to photograph the last event?

If someone had asked me, I would not have allowed any photographer—daughter or son—anywhere near our spiraling inward to spiral back out again.

While others talked to the hunk and tried to clue him in to the day, I was in the hallway talking to a daughter with cashew-colored skin. She told me that she was a peacemaker in her class. She was clearly more mature than many of her age mates. We talked about what she liked in school—choir—and what she did not. She asked what needed to be done to transform the room then being used for creating a journal of statements about why girls are great into a room where one-hundred-some daughters could dance. I told her what we needed to do: fold and move over fifty chairs and fifteen tables. Collect all the statements and art supplies.

She said, "Humm, that will be hard."

"It will be quicker than we think if we all chip in," I said.

Then we made it so.

It did not occur to me at the time to stop everything and usher the hunk away. He was sequestered in a side room with several of the other presenters. I must have assumed they were handling him.

The spiral dance was not a spectator event; it was not a show, though the photographer's presence made it so. And many daughters were deprived of their immersions in the movement and the moments of daughter-centered intimacy as they instead turned to the only him with a camera in the room and smiled.

The spiral was turning inward, inward, with the instruction that we look at each other's faces. And there, in the circle's center, was a man, the first of the day, and his camera, a most intrusive third eye. All the elder and younger daughter twosomes in the room had spent some time considering the effect of media images on their perceptions. I wondered what the image of the hunk and his camera brought to mind.

With hindsight, it is clear that I was asked to be some sort of entertainment, to end the day with a bang! The organizers asked me to offer the girls an exciting closure of their day. Yes, I was asked to lead a visually interesting event and, *of course!* the pictures of the spiral dance were delicious.

But nobody asked me if taking pictures of the dance would be appropriate.

And the newspaper sent a man.

We spiraled into the man with the camera in the middle. He was not in the middle when we began, but soon after we began he slipped in between the bodies of elder and younger daughters, many of whom were looking at him rather than each other.

We were spiraling in, but the outside world had its camera eye on us.

The eye of the becameraed man claimed the face-on energy of a girl with her belly button showing. She was visibly pleased by his presence and attention. Her beaming image adorned the local newspaper's article about the day. She said having her picture taken was the greatest thing that happened for her.

In my Momma's words, I thought it was a *sin and disgrace* to have a man with a camera in the focal point of our closing spiral.

But, apparently, it was great for the girls to be the subjects of an admiring cameraman. At the end of the day so many of the daughters stopped and posed for the hunk. I yelled at him, again, and again, to get out of the center of the spiral.

We were not gathered, stoking the energy of these daughters, to wind themselves around him. The spiral wound tighter and tighter, closer and closer together, almost stagnating, until he dropped to the floor and rolled out of the middle, through the moving feet of daughters and their elders. I felt completely absurd encouraging daughters to chant the chant we created to celebrate girls' greatness while interrupting my own chanting to scream a man out of the center of the daughters' circling.

As long as the photographer clicked his camera away in the middle of the circle, we could not turn around. I had doubt at my elbow, in the form of a colleague experiencing her first spiral dance and thinking I couldn't wind us out. As I yelled at the photographer to get Out!, *Out!* of the center, she yelled back, "We don't know how."

My energy and attention were divided between deepening the daughters in the power of keeping together in time and needing to get the man with the camera out of the middle of our power-filled creation.

Apparently, this bears repeating:

As long as there was a man with a camera in the middle of the circle, the daughters could not turn around.

As long as there was a man with a camera in the middle of the circle, the line of elder and younger daughters could not spiral completely in and focus on each other's faces and spiral magically, powerfully outward again.

Don't do this in your hometown.

Remember this story, elder daughters, as you work and plan to serve younger daughters; remember.

Remember this story, younger daughters, and ask your elders to allow you some experiences of learning about your greatness outside of the camera's altering glare.

Remember this story, men, truly loving fathers and brothers and sons of daughters. Remember this story, holders of cameras. What daughters do in your presence is not the same as what we would do out of your vision and clicking third eyes.

Remember, remember to attend to resonance of thought, word, and deed, passion and action, commitment and reflection.

And, please, divine daughter sisters, if you ever witness me in moments of forgetfulness, remind me.

all someday mothers
of daughters
of sons

VOW

Mothers
You gave what
You got. I shall not

Honey
Hush daughters
God-privilege sons

You gave
What you got
Fathers. I shall not

BECOMING HEARTICULATE

THERE IS SOME ELEMENT of Life within us that knows the most articulate, compassionate interaction possible within each moment. In many spiritual traditions, the human embodiment of this wisdom source has been considered the anatomical heart or center of the chest. In secular terms, an understanding that our hearts are a source of articulate compassion is evident in such American slang as "speaking from the heart" or "getting to the heart of the matter." Similarly, the innermost, juiciest, and therefore strongest wood in a tree is called the heartwood.

By being hearticulate, I cultivate the skills I need to be true to my vows . . . *I shall not / honey hush daughters* . . .

To be hearticulate, lend your heart your tongue. This implies opening the h*eart*'s middle *ear,* hearing, then giving v ɔice to the depths of Life from the depths of your being. It is possible to do this in the midst of all kinds of chaotic carrying on.

Practice helps make it possible to consistently give voice to Life. The spontaneous freedom with which this wisdom arises is energetically related to the audacious honesty of children's voices before they are socialized into silence. Being hearticulate adds a compassionate maturity of being and perception to a childlike lack of verbal restraint.

Ironically, it seems easiest to begin practicing hearticulation while embroiled in an ongoing, heart-rending conflict. While both beauty and devastation can break the heart open, in my life, devastation has been a more reliable motivator for developing the skill of being hearticulate.

There are two prerequisites to developing hearticulation in the face of adversity. First, you need to feel some measure of commitment to something or someone involved in the interaction in order to stay motivated enough to listen with the heart's middle ear. You also need to drop all investment in being "right." Being hearticulate is less about being right or wrong than it is about being open to the multidimensional truths of each moment.

Adversity is such a good context in which to begin your training in hearticulation because it offers abundant opportunities to notice the difference between how you feel when your heart is open and how you feel when it is closed. Hearticulation requires an open heart, a quality of attention in which the ability to perceive clearly and interact with any person or situation is not obscured by conceptualizations, judgments, desires, or aversions. In other words, being of open heart gives you access to the depth of wisdom on which hearticulation is based.

How do you know when your heart is open? Try this experiment. Imagine a person who reliably gets on your last nerve. When you merely think about this person, your jaws get tight. Now imagine opening your heart in her or his presence. Notice how the center of your chest feels.

What happened? Did the mere intention of opening your heart in the presence of a difficult person bring up a sense of resistance in your body, emotions, or mind? Did an inner voice question my intelligence for suggesting such a stupid action as being openhearted in the presence of someone around whom your heart habitually hurts?

Perhaps you were fortunate enough to experience a bit of relief, no matter how subtle, from a habitual tightness (suffering) at the mere thought or image of an adversary. This relief is a kind of freedom. This relief is also a gift of the open heart.

This simple exercise illuminates the essence of how to practice being openhearted. First, you bring a heightened awareness to the center of your chest or to your anatomical heart. Then you intend to be of open heart. Notice: I didn't say to open your heart. This practice activates the powers of intention and imagination to affect our physiology.

Even if the place of openness is only metaphorically located in the heart, setting your intention and focusing it on a location helps cultivate the skills of hearticulation. Being of open heart implies an effortless return to a natural state of being. I experience the openhearted state as more effortless, less of an energy drain, than more constricted states of being.

Contrast openheartedness with the state of being that accompanies the desire for approval. I've grappled with this desire often while writing this book. In seeking your approval, I expend considerable energy trying to guess what words, imagery, and concepts you will think are intelligent or, better still, elegantly expressed. Then I must stifle all forms of expression that don't match what I think you will consider worthy of respect.

Keeping my attention focused on being as hearticulate as possible is much simpler and requires much less energy than the guesswork of trying to impress you enough to win your approval.

I risk the awkwardness of hyper-self-consciousness about our shared activity—you as reader, me as writer of these words—in order to flesh out the motivations of becoming hearticulate.

Why practice being hearticulate? What are the benefits? Peace, both internal and external, is one of the greatest blessings of hearticulation.

The quality of attention honed by being of open heart is somehow calming. Being of open heart seems to bring with it a liberating disengagement from reactive responses. This gives wisdom some wiggle room with which to influence a given situation. While it isn't clear which comes first, peace or wisdom, it is clear that they are at least twins, perhaps identical ones.

I feel a subtle need to defend the value of peacefulness. A small voice inside says, "Peace is fine, but what about all that is not peaceful in this world?" I answer this voice: "Hearticulate people are often moved by compassion to be balancing influences in the world's internal and external messes."

The practice of being hearticulate begins when we amplify quiet wisdom's influence in our lives. This is not to say that loud wisdom doesn't have its place. But the focus of becoming hearticulate is to amplify the voices of wisdom presently being shouted down by other voices we have internalized.

Here I am thinking particularly about the voice of NOstopCAN'T-don'tNOT, a voice so many women internalize and treat as the voice of an all-powerful God. You probably know this voice, though I hope not too intimately. Still, I'm sure that if you're a woman, you've heard this voice and spoken this voice at least once as you've moved to create an expression of your heart's wisdom in the world. I think here of the community I long for but have yet to create in which to explore complementary health care approaches to thriving with uterine fibroids. I think here of the divine daughters' council I long for but have yet to create, a council organized around compassionate awareness and a devotion to Life-centered maturity.

The voice of NOstopCAN'Tdon'tNOT has told me I cannot simultaneously complete this book and do the organizational and emotional work involved in helping to create the ongoing communities and councils of my dreams. Writing this, I wonder if this voice is actually a voice of wisdom in this instance. *Yes,* I hear in answer to my question. In this instance, the voice of NOstopCAN'Tdon'tNOT*now* is wise.

I remember bringing out my first recording, *Reach Across the Lines,* which contains the title song, another original song, "Freedom Is Just a Yes Away," and a solo rendition of "The Friendship Train," in which I simultaneously sing the parts of Gladys Knight and the Pips. *Reach Across the Lines* was created to be used on college campuses in trainings in transforming racism.

Shortly after its release, I was invited to play it at a Women Against Racism conference in Iowa. All I had to do was identify myself to the deejay, and she would fill the room with my music.

I walked in and, from a safe, anonymous distance, watched the deejay jamming to a Tracy Chapman tune. Immediately a chorus of NOstopCAN'Tdon'tNOT kicked in.

"These women won't enjoy what I've done," the chorus sang. "It doesn't compare to Tracy's work." (That is, it doesn't compare favorably.) "They'll make fun of me when they find out I did this recording. It's not danceable enough."

Heeding the council of NOstopCAN'Tdon'tNOT and allowing the fears it fanned to get the best of me, I watched the deejay closely and stifled another voice advising me to introduce myself to her and tell her which cut I thought the crowd of partying women would enjoy. As soon as she took a break, which I knew she eventually would, given the sweat she worked up dancing pert' near nonstop for about an hour, I slipped behind the table, snatched my recording out of the stack of others waiting to be played, and ran to the bathroom, feeling simultaneously triumphant and totally self-defeated.

I held my voice back from the community in and for which *Reach Across the Lines* was created. These women were my friends and colleagues, for Life's sake. Yet the voice of NOstopCAN'Tdon'tNOT convinced me to hold *Reach* back from them.

This less-than-hearticulate episode happened long before I began to practice being hearticulate. Being hearticulate brings me a sense of courage as well as a sense of peace. The peace includes a noncoercive coexistence with self- and Life-limiting voices. The courage to act upon heartfelt creative impulses grows stronger as the self-sabotaging voices of fear are heard for what they are.

Being hearticulate first came alive for me at a time in my creative life that seemed to be both the best and worst of times. Outwardly, I seemed to be enjoying an enviable success: my dream of being a member of Bobby McFerrin's Voicestra had come true, and we were performing all over, appearing on late-night and early-morning talk shows. Relatives I didn't even know I had started showing up at performances or calling and writing to congratulate me on my success or to chide me for not staying in closer touch.

At home, all was less than well. Because I was away so much, my husband, Martin, bore more than his share of our responsibility as resident fellows for 129 students living in Ujamaa, the African American focus house at Stanford University. Voicestra's national media exposure brought with it a measure of local celebrity. Increasingly, our students and colleagues would greet Martin by asking, "How's Rachel? I saw her on . . ." and never quite get around to inquiring about his welfare.

Simultaneously, Martin's research on the expression of anger at work was proceeding with difficulty. He was daring to explore questions about anger and organizational behavior that hadn't been asked before in the research literature. This pioneering work brought with it the suffering most groundbreakers experience, that of having to prove the issue is worth exploring. Further, without precedents, he faced unusual challenges in designing the research.

We stepped into a stereotypical conflict for contemporary, high-achievement couples: she was enjoying more success than he was. Support roles and expectations ran counter to the cultural norm, and he was secretly angry about it.

A long-standing failure to cooperate in dealing with troubling sexual dynamics preceding and born of our relationship simmered underneath the other tensions. I entered therapy to free myself from a post-traumatic stress syndrome born of sexual abuse, but Martin treated our sexual troubles as only my problem.

Riding the joy-filled world of vocal creativity, I would sing and dance myself into ecstasies with the Stras daily. It was excruciating that my relationship with Martin did not cultivate the energy thus generated. My erotic health—which at the time I thought meant mutually satisfying heterosexual sex—suffered. It seemed somehow unnatural to be in a relationship of the depth I enjoyed with Martin even then, while experiencing such a debilitating lack of sexual intimacy that I was driven more than once to the edge of disastrous affairs.

I tired of addressing our difficulties by talking, talking, talking. I need more energy, I'd say. Let me show you how I like it, I'd say. After years of frustration with gentler approaches and years of Martin's defensive responses, I became bitey fierce in our increasingly infrequent sexual encounters.

One day I came home from the road, there was no food I could eat in the house, the car smelled of some strange perfume, and Martin was angry.

Martin was angry and then not in bed at 3 A.M. When I went out to see what troubled him enough to get him up (he usually slept so soundly), he told me he needed to talk to me about coming to care deeply for another.

"You're having an affair," I hollered. "I hate you I hate you I hate you!"

I continued yelling until Martin screamed back at me, "You never listen to me!"

Then he was up and beating on the closet doors, and I was up and quietly terrified, turning on every light I could find and saying, "I want us both to see clearly what's going on. I don't want you to hurt yourself, and I don't want you to hurt me."

The next day I began asking Martin about his parents' relationship and digging around in his bringings up for clues to his behavior. It became clearer than ever to me that we needed help if we were going to stay together. It became clear to me that even if we were going to break up, we needed help with the intergenerational dynamics the breakdown in our relationship revealed.

Healing was what mattered most to me.

It also mattered that his lover was a white woman. It mattered that weeks before, I had broken down in tears about how his refusal also to get help was hurting me. It mattered that he said he heard me but didn't. It mattered that he majored in psychology but didn't receive the counsel of the discipline to which he devoted so much of his time. It mattered that he treated my struggle back to embodied sanity as my struggle alone.

It mattered that I am older than he is and that the women in my family have a tradition of marrying younger men. It mattered. It mattered that I had made it through three years of law school and had passed the bar and had provided leadership for a number of projects at Stanford. It mattered that I was the woman and that he was the man. It mattered that I made more money than he did, though neither of us made much. I heard him when he said, "*I'm supposed* to be smarter than you and make more money," and we laughed and I thought he was joking.

It mattered that he came from a family of only sons, only brothers. It mattered that he went to a pricey prep school and then an ivy league college before coming to Stanford. It mattered that he was used to being "the one."

It mattered that the woman he managed to have sex with thrice in ten days was white and that he did it while I was away. He said his lover accepted him as he was. I told him she didn't even know him. It mattered that, at the time, I didn't really understand how unaccepting I had been of Martin.

It mattered that I thought I had done all in my power to unlock my body and feelings about what was hurting us. It mattered that I didn't really understand how unaccepting I was of myself. It mattered that I was committed to doing all in my power to simultaneously salvage my dignity and save our marriage. It mattered that I thought about more than us when I told him we needed to stay together at least until the end of the year: Ujamaa, ravaged the year before by national media attention to racial incidents, needed our solidarity.

It mattered that our lives were not entirely our own, that I was motivated to stay together for 129 young adults: somebody else's daughters and sons. Whose lives belong only to their cells, untouched and untouching of others? It mattered that I was aware enough to want to learn something useful from the hell we were going through. It mattered that I was aware of the damage I worked to get out from under while simultaneously answering Life's many calls to create words and music, community and a sense of inner safety.

But what mattered most of all was my desire to heal and be healed.

When I talked to Martin about all that mattered to me, it became clear that he didn't think anything he studied about repression or psychological therapy applied to him. He refused to see a counselor about what was going on between us. He was raging and angry and hurt and unwilling to listen to anything I suggested about needing help.

Lacking Martin's cooperation and driven by shame to hide our situation from friends and family, I turned to a mute yet reliable source of solace: books. I browsed the shelves of Two Sisters, my then-local women's bookstore, in search of healing partners.

The Enlightened Heart, edited by Stephen Mitchell, was the first book to fall off the shelf into my hand, literally. I opened it to Mitchell's translation of "Psalm 1" from the Hebrew and Christian scriptures. This poem reassured me that the woman and the man who *no longer nourish illusions* and *keep their hearts open, day and night* were blessed.

The next book I consulted, *A Book for Couples,* by Hugh and Gayle Prather, suggested that this problem of an affair was really no different in origin than any other relationship problem, no bigger deal, no harder to resolve. This book suggested that the adversarial couple begin to heal their alienation from each other by openheartedly reviewing their relationship daily.

Of this I was sure: I truly loved Martin. There was and is something about his quality of heart that makes my own sing. On our best days, which are most days these days, we answer each other's unspoken questions as though we were in verbal communication. He'll think about asking me when I'd like to have dinner, and I'll say out loud, "Let's eat as soon as I'm finished editing this page." This level of communion was present even during our troubled times; it was just covered over with our immaturity, gender conflicts, and every unresolved relationship that we had brought along with us.

Right next to the mess we were in, I felt a profound loving respect for Martin and a conviction that if we could make it to the other side of this one, we could enjoy an enduring, mutually nourishing relationship.

Either way, I was unwilling to walk away before deeply understanding my contributions to the trouble troubling us. I came home that day and told Martin as much, told him that I felt a power of love between us that I wanted to preserve. I confessed not knowing precisely what I needed to do differently to heal the gaping wounds between us, but that I wanted to. My willingness to change was not unconditional, however.

I had three conditions for staying in our relationship, which I wanted to do at least until the end of the year for the sake of the students in Ujamaa and for our own sakes. First, his affair had to end immediately. Second, he had to enter a therapeutic relationship to help him deal with his repressed rage. Third, each morning, as our first action of shared consciousness, we would have what has become our ongoing practice of heart-time.

Try this at home.

During heart-time, we take turns speaking and listening to each other. While one of us speaks, the other only listens—no questions, no commentary. The speaker responds to this question: how is your heart?

Both of us also vow to keep our hearts open, no matter what. If either partner's heart feels closed, the process stops until both hearts feel open again.

The first time it was my turn to listen, I was shocked by how strange it felt to have my heart open in Martin's presence. When it was my turn to speak, I told him of my discovery and begged his forgiveness. The profound honesty of our first heart-time, and my admissions of error, convinced Martin of my sincere desire to transform our marriage. He credits the structure of heart-time for giving him a safety and respect that he didn't otherwise feel. In heart-time, I could, *finally,* hear the truth in Martin's words, "I wear my heart on my sleeve all the time," and "You never really listen to me." He was justifiably angry about my arrogant disregard of his feelings and opinions. He was relieved by my demonstrated promise to change.

We'd been together almost seven years when we began heart-time. The legacy of the seven-year-itch was not lost on me. Nor was I pleased to meet the characters who showed up and did their level best to shut my heart or hurl daggers out of my mouth when it was Martin's turn to talk. A veritable tall, thin, corps of pale, male judges in black and white robes regularly showed up, as did a woman with a whip in her hands. I cajoled them into making appointments during which we could speak later, later, not now. This I did silently after asking Martin to be patient with me while I worked to reopen my heart.

As often as not, I revealed these characters as soon as I could do so without allowing their personae to control my actions and words. Long-held resentments and repressed emotions of all sorts held themselves up shamefully and shamelessly before us. Day after day, we kept our vow to open our hearts and learn about ourselves and each other as we talked.

I don't remember when the general tone of heart-time moved from one of primarily healing deep difficulties to being more energizing or downright entertaining. Even during the difficult times it was often entertaining. The image of three white-robed, white, male judges springs ridiculously to mind as I think about the many times of laughter during heart-time. They appeared as an unholy trinity, three thin lines of tightly clustered crackpots. Their collective, emaciated huddle was echoed in their individual body postures. One always had his arms tightly folded across his chest. Another hunched his shoulders, balled up his fist, fumed. The one in the middle just peered over his glasses with a look of disapproval that seemed practiced to perfection.

These judges were as likely to appear when I was the speaker as when I was the listener. As listener, I sometimes felt their presence as cotton in my ears, sometimes as a maniacal jabbering that made listening to Martin impossible. They also shrieked their disapproval of what I was about to say. Sometimes it felt as though they were loading my tongue with lethal weapons to prepare my response to something Martin had uttered in innocence, vulnerability, and trust.

When I first noticed their almost constant companionship, it took tremendous energy to keep my heart open in their presence. Which came first, the sensation of my heart closing or the perception that the tribunal was standing on my chest? I never knew, yet I learned quickly that whenever the judges appeared, I needed to call time-out and tend to my heart, even if their heart-closing influence was so subtle as to be barely sensed.

It is essential here to focus on their voice-snatching manifestation. Remember the core heart-time agreement that all speaking and listening stops if either partner's heart begins to feel like it's closing. Initially, during my frequent interruptions to deal with the judges' jabbering, I would negotiate silently with them, promise to listen to them after heart-time was over, offer them an extended, luxury vacation in a community they loved to criticize. Later, as both Martin and I became more trusting of being openhearted with each other and ourselves, I often negotiated out loud.

It somehow strengthened our relationship to bring the tribunal to light. Doing so transformed an initial tongue-snatching dynamic into an occasion to restore my voice. This requires some teasing out here. I initially negotiated with the judges in silence because what came out of their mouths was heinous to me. Their judgments were never complimentary, never, "Oh, Martin, how wonderful that you are aware of that dynamic between us." Never, "Rachel, see how far you must have come to be able to talk about this without ripping Martin to shreds with your teeth."

The tribunal specialized in destructive criticism. Just listening to them made me sick. And their persistence, their litanies of Martin's incompetencies and my stupidity for colluding in being victimized, seemed to have a dangerous ring of partial truth. They were judges, after all. In the United States, judges receive the training of lawyers, a training that my tenure as a Stanford law student taught me includes sifting through voluminous amounts of information, selecting the bit that most supports a desired outcome, and presenting it in the most persuasive light possible.

Judges come to their positions through a process rife with the tactics (and pitfalls) of persuasion. Their appointments, whether by vote or by pleasure of an elected official, are political. Enough people, or an important enough person, must be convinced that a judge-to-be's mastery of persuasion renders her or him immune to undue influence. Otherwise, the judge would not be able to mediate hearings and arrive at just resolutions of conflicts, despite lawyers' expensively manipulated performances aimed at resolving the conflict in their own client's favor.

The question then arises: who assigned the thin, white tribunal to the task of keeping my heart and mouth shut? Speculating about the roots of their existence didn't bring me closer to kicking them out of office or persuading them to retire. I called them judges because of the robes and funny hats they wore. Writing this, I now realize their behavior was more like that of lawyers. For whom were they advocates? Whom did they oppose?

The questions themselves were liberating. I did not need to answer them in order to reap their potential for liberation. Each time I confronted the judges, whether silently or out loud, their hold on my tongue became that much less powerful. Their voices grew less perceptible, and their images disappeared after a while. I can't remember the last heart-time I actually saw them. But the dynamic they advocated so powerfully, the arrogant attitude that Martin was incompetent and required my instruction in the fine arts of restorative relationship, still arises when we discover some difference between us that tempts me to label Martin's way wrong and mine right.

Tussling with an extreme form of being judgmental has tuned my perceptions to its more subtle manifestations. Working with the judges was somehow like lifting weights in that I developed a strength of perceptive ability in the process. It was also akin to singing scales or chanting daily in order to develop trust in my vocal flexibility and in the ability to sound in the outer world what is first heard in my heart.

Why do Martin and I continue to practice heart-time daily? Because it begins our day with the tone of peace, of authenticity, of listening deeply and speaking just as deeply and truthfully. We practice because the practice nourishes and protects our abilities to be in restorative relations with each other and with our lives.

What does any of this have to do with the needs of poor children or the unrelenting fact of domestic violence in the United States? How does my wide-open heart help transform the most heinous norms of our times and cultures?

To harm another requires a rending in our relations with Life. Violently harming another is evidence of diminished humanity. People who are lethally violent are called cold-blooded murderers and hardened criminals. On the continuum of violence, I have seen internal images of myself with dagger in hand, with tongue poised as weapon, capable of shredding my beloved into psychological bits. Earlier in our relationship, I flew into a rage over his insensitivity and punched a hole in the wall of our cottage. Violence is violence.

Violence begets violence.

It is a fact that I suffered sexual violence at the hands of several men and in the attitudes of my parents and our culture. It is also a fact that my internalization of that violence has diminished both my creative engagement with the world at large and my ability to be effective in the face of ongoing injustices.

Somewhere in my open heart I find the courageous capacity to stand up and speak up for the silenced without passing the violence on. All are required: standing up, speaking, and skillfully transforming the very violence that our species seems hypnotized into believing social transformation demands.

There must be at least one other way to address our legacy of wounding ourselves and one another, some other way to live than that which destroys the Life we cannot live without. Devoting moments each morning to heart-time has given me the forum in which to quest for other lived experiences of strength.

Heart-time has taught me that I don't have to attack someone else's integrity in order to affirm my own. In fact, the degree to which I listen and speak in attack mode has a direct, negative correlation to my ability to listen and speak for a more restorative alternative. If social transformation is our commitment, then we must transform the frameworks through which we look at the troubles of our worlds. Clearly, our old ways of doing things have not yet eradicated our most tenacious woes. Girl babies the world over are still left outside to die or suffer sexual abuse under the bodies of relatives and so-called family friends. The ravages of racism continue to be closely connected to economic and demographic conditions. Proposals for improving the quality of life for people in "developing" countries often disconnect the people from the Life of indigenous and ecological cultures.

If actions motivated by anger and hardheartedness had any long-term restorative effects, then our species would have returned to harmonious coexistence with our Earthly neighbors long ago. But anyone who has witnessed a fire knows that fire burns itself out. So do many of the changes wrought by heartless anger.

Moments a morning, allow yourself to experiment with another way: becoming hearticulate.

THE FREE JAZZ OF DISHWASHING

A FTER WE EAT WHAT WE'VE GROWN and it begins to grow into us, I get up from Momma's kitchen table, run water in the sink, and begin to clean a day's worth of dirty dishes. In this moment, I belong to a daughterhood of dish cleaners living all over the world.

Some daughters use sand to scour ancient metal pots. Others use the gifts of a nearby body of water, a washing hole, a small pond, a stream.

step into this stream of music
sing what you hear . . .

Many daughters are blessed to enjoy their after-meal task together. They laugh as they clean, perhaps they even have a song, perhaps many songs, a repertoire for cleaning dirty dishes. Other daughters work alone, like I do, in what some dare call more civilized homes, in settings more isolated then those graced by the wild's communal order.

Some daughters work outside, cleaning up after the family meal, accompanied by symphonies of crickets, screech owls, water running free, the *swoosh, swoosh* of sand rhythmically making dishes clean. Other daughters are encased, as I am, in metal, stone, and wood, locked behind airtight windows in the winter, our hands covered in rubber or plastic gloves to protect our fingers from the caustic cleaning chemicals we use.

For some the sounds and tasks of cleaning dirty dishes is a joy-filled part of our communal being. For others, as it was for me for all too long, the music of cleaning up after the meal is unheard.

"You do this because you're the girl," Momma said, the doing and being simultaneously seen as a blessing—according of the light in Momma's eyes—and heard as curse. It took me nearly thirty years of washing dirty dishes before I heard the music of the task.

These sounds accompany dish cleaning: the rhythmic slapping of sand on metal, the *ching* of spatula meeting spoon, the drum of spoon on clay. The free-jazz-like play of what we call inanimate objects singing out, *think again, think again,* polyrhythmically.

Yet, without thinking, when washing dishes we are living elements of chant: *breath,* we are breathing; *rhythm and repetition* of water and sand transforming the dirty into the clean for millennia through an infinite number of daughters' hands; *intention,* the aftermath of our actions clearly known: cleanliness, order; *tone,* the swooshing and clinging and thump and slosh and slap and our own songs' tones, if we're lucky.

If we're lucky to be working outside in the warmth, the night birds' singing serenades us. Stars witness our rendition of an infinite, always-after-meal activity: classical in having stood the test of time. Musical, our managing of mess.

The dull sounds of plastic plate clicking against plastic plate after a campfire meal. The metal of pot against pot, the ringing of fine china, the wineglasses singing, the aluminum pie tin drum, sans sweet potato pie, the many fired clay bowls, the wooden spoons all adding texture to sanitation's symphony.

Amidst domestically orchestrated sonority—harmonic, rhythmic, or not—accompanied by voices or wrapped in a solitary silence, there are daughters. Our hands are instruments of continuity, cleanliness, and service. Some of our lips are sealed; others are singing in joy or protest of our lot.

I am singing as I wash the dirty dishes in my Momma's narrow kitchen, a room so small, so narrow, it cannot accommodate two of me arm-to-outstretched-arm. I wash the dishes to help my mother; to give her a time to rest. She is eighty something. She is tired. Her short-term memory flies around the room. I have asked for peace and quiet so that I can focus on the lessons of the day, peace so that I can just have some quiet now, Momma. The day has been filled with the pokings and proddings of examinations, many blood tests, a suspicious mammogram, and questions Momma keeps forgetting to ask her doctors. In the hospital, I am her long-distance memory. I am her advocate, telling the second medical resident who steps into the room that my Momma says she will be examined only by the *regular* doctor. I ask for the *Physicians' Desk Reference* to learn about possible side effects of Momma's prescribed blood pressure medicine. I ask for less stressful alternatives.

At home, I advocate for myself. I ask Momma to stop talking for a moment as I wash dishes at the end of the day so that I can finally have some peace while she rests.

One moment, Momma is silent. The next moment she forgets what I have asked for and begins to jabber on about how grateful she is for all I've done and when am I leaving and why so soon? I turn to her and I say, again, Momma please, may I have some quiet now, please? I need some peace. She doesn't mean to disrespect my needs. She's just excited that I am here, here to visit her clear down out of snowy New Hampshire.

We breathe together. She sits and I stand in the house of my childhood. She purchased this house soon after arriving in Philadelphia from South Carolina. Momma's house, this bricked-in narrowness, is our meeting ground. This place, where I now beg for peace, is where we first became each other's: Momma, daughter, Mommasitter, daughterlove. *Glory be.*

To respect my request for quiet, Momma must leave the room. She cannot, it seems, bear for us to be in each other's company and be quiet. What I seek is not sensed by her as an opportunity for shared grace. How I long for the peace of a Momma near me and peace filled and both of us just silent and nourished by the hush. But peace in Momma's house frequently costs me the loss of her presence.

I have the kitchen to myself. The task of cleaning up, the task that I abhorred as a girl because it wasn't shared by my brother, is now a source of joy and restorative silence. I face, with some measure of grace, my failed attempts to avoid traditional daughterly duties. I am still a girl, I am still my Momma's baby, grown-up, taller, but still the only girl my Momma has.

She told me this would be so, no matter how tall I got.

Remember, I'm the Mommy, she said, when I had to stop measuring my height by where the top of my head rested on my Momma's body: waist, shoulders, forehead. It happened quickly one year, before I graduated from the third grade: we started measuring my height by where the top of Momma's head rested on me.

We both remember she is the Mommy. She still calls me sweetheart. She still calls me baby and doll. Her calls come for me, not for my brother who lives in the same city, to help care for certain aspects of her agedness. As it usually is with the daughters of elderly people all over the world, *the girl* is called home.

I sanctify the inevitable. Here I am, here I be in my Momma's kitchen, happy to serve her as she has served countless other daughters and sons who call her Miz Bagby. The service that I happily do is complex. There are struggles. There is, yes, the pain of seeing her snaky ways of adapting to being a strong woman in a culture still enthralled by the so-called powers of men and their privilege of being direct. There is the pain of recognizing, at the writing of this paragraph, that part of me is still enthralled by the stories that degrade snaky wisdom.

But that is another story. In the now of Momma's kitchen, I am alone. Momma is gone. Usually, at this time of day, the television would blast at me from the living room as Dad turns it higher and higher to accommodate his elder hearing. But there is rare silence in the house. Momma is no longer in the kitchen jougging at me, jougging at me with her questions of when I am leaving and where I have to go next and what my work is and how my husband is faring without me. I am here and blessedly alone.

In the quiet of Momma's kitchen, for the first time since I can remember, a wordless chant spontaneously rises up out of my mouth. The very impulse of singing out spontaneously in Momma's domain surprises me. I hesitate for a moment to acknowledge the rarity of the impulse, *Here, you bid me sing you here?*, before joyfully surrendering to a quality of singing that sanctifies my lot.

I give in to vocal sounding accompanied by enameled cast iron pots that ring out as I ping a spatula against them. The rhythm of the pots' ringing turns into a beat. The pots and I are joined by the sounds of aged plates and bowls. Even in their chipped glory, they make fine percussive instruments.

I sing as I negotiate the furniture cluttered around the kitchen table. I kick the short step stool that Momma uses to put her iron pots away. Kicked, the stool sounds like the hi-hat of a trap drum set. I kick the stool again. Moving the wooden high stool that Momma sits on as she washes the dishes adds a snaring texture to the sound.

Now everything that shuffles moves into this chant that moves into my body and out of my mouth from only Life knows where.

This moment is a blessing. It is my joy to ease Momma's elder years. I feel privileged to help her, to serve a Momma who has served generations of people too poor to move out of a neighborhood that has yet to fully recover from the riots that followed the assassination of Martin Luther King, Jr., in 1968. I love Momma's good heart and aging body out loud.

Her loving intentions toward me shine brightly beyond all daughterly conditioning. And I am able to serve her lovingly to the depth and degree that I am free of resentment about the conditioning that stifled us both. This I know, bone deep. And my bones are ringing with a joy that surprises me out loud, in the form of freedom singing through this moment in my body and in my Momma's crowded kitchen. Life, have mercy.

I am dancing with each chair. Each stool, each bit of furniture previously experienced as inhibiting my breathing, is now my friend. I serenade the occasional audience of baby cockroaches offa my last nerve. I sing the dishes clean. I am happy and loud and singing and surprised and remembering and transforming stifling vocal habits born and, in the moment, dying, in my Momma's kitchen.

Daddy is home, yet the television is not on and things change, *Glory Be, Glory Be.* Momma is home and not at me, and Nelson, the privileged one, the precious son, my brother, no longer calls Momma's home his own. He finally, sometime after the age of forty, married another woman other than my Momma and now lives somewhere else with an unborrowed wife. Praise Life.

The Life song pouring out of my mouth, singing, surprising, and blessing me, brings healing upon healing. Voice blessings ring out through my Momma's kitchen now. Here, I am coming into a stronger, more assertive and spontaneous tongue. Here, washing dishes, where I finally know I am not the only girl, not the only daughter in the world washing dirty dishes, Life is singing freely through my being and my voice is free.

Now the voice also rises in the midst of this change, in the moment-to-moment call and possibility of freedom. The voice rises and blesses this moment with awareness, with query, with singing, with gift, with assertiveness, with asking, with prayer for understanding, prayer for listening, with opinions, with consideration, with the undoing of the silencing, with the standing up for emotions, with the fullness of Life-restoring tones.

Now, during the baptism of water that the plates and the pots, the spoons and the forks and the knives each receive daily, I am baptizing freedom, singing our daughterhoods free in the kitchen in my Momma's house, in the holiness in our bodies breathing, protected by narrow brick walls.

And all 'round this planet, the home upon which we all make our homes, this place of gravity, atmosphere, oxygen, water, fire, fruits, and grains, around the Earth, daughter after daughter puts her hand to the cleaning of that which holds what we eat to sustain ourselves, and in the course of cleaning, a round of blessing our shared living begins again.

And the Earth turns on its axis, a motion echoed in the circling of a cleaning cloth around a soiled bowl.

Imagine a chorus of gratitude arising from each of our mouths as we each in turn sing ourselves clean, sing praises of the cleaning as cyclical as the sun rising and falling; illuminating the moon's phases of wasting and growth. Imagine receiving our cycles of eating, of use, and of cleaning as domestic blessings, equitably shared by both daughters and sons. *Glory, glory, glory.*

still

REST

Excerpt from "Rest,"
written by Rachel Bagby. Copyright
1993 Breathing Music ASCAP.
Used by permission.

REST IN TRUTH. Rest in Health. Rest in Focus. Rest in
Balance. Rest in Work.

To rest in Truth is to retrieve all the energy required to
maintain and live lies. To rest in Health renders unnecessary the
extraordinary efforts that the treatment of illnesses demands. This is
true whether the illness be of the body, the mind, the emotions, the
spirit, the soul, or the community. These illnesses include the delusion that we cannot rest in the ample lap of Life's grandmothering.

Resting in Focus offers the gifts of unscattered energies. Balance
rests first this side, then that. That which is balanced wears well.
Resting in Work can make work feel effortless because it is focused,
because it is not a lie, because there is give-and-take: balance. Rest in
Work allows time for reflection, pacing, and asking, "Is this enough?"

Let us Rest our eyes now, daughter sisters. We are enough.

SEE COLOR

"**I** KNOW YOU PROBABLY mean well, but do you tell *white* peo-ple you've just met that you're color-blind?" Marva asked.

The dark-rooted blond to whom she spoke sat back as if the question ever so gently guided and then held her erect in her seat. A flight attendant locked his beverage cart in place beside the two women's row. Leaning over Marva, he placed a napkin on the blond's tray. "Something to drink?" he asked.

"Hot water; I have my own tea bag," she said.

"And you, ma'am?"

Marva waved the flight attendant away. She put her left elbow up on the armrest and cradled her chin in her hand. She glanced at her watch, noting the sixty-three seconds that passed before her aisle mate stopped fiddling with her tea and said, "I didn't mean I don't see color; of course I see color. Your skin looks beautiful against what you're wearing." She smiled. Marva didn't. "What I mean is we're—"

"—all human, right?" Marva asked. "Listen Jennifer Dalton—"

"Please, call me Jen. My friends call me Jen."

"Jennifer, listen," Marva said. "Despite what you say you mean, it sounds like you're saying human doesn't come in my hue."

Water slowly filling Jennifer's eyes made them look more and more like the kind of blues Marva could barely breathe around. Something terrible and familiar in the way Jennifer's eyes grabbed at Marva's face made her turn away in search of an empty seat on the other side of the plane.

Not another one, not the second one in three short days, Marva said to herself. I thought this girl saw me as her peer, not a stand-in for someCOLOREDone else she misses or wants.

The plane hit an air pocket. Both women held their stomachs as the turbulence tousled them against each other. When the lurching finally stopped, the captain's blaring reassurances made conversation impossible. Marva, grateful for the interruptions, spent the time considering her next move.

She could withdraw into a haven of sleep and reading. She could ignore the part of herself angered by what some would consider an innocent ignorance. She could condition her interaction on reciprocity: I'll be your black stand-in if you'll be my white one. Every option Marva considered made the polyrhythmic pulsing in her stomach worse. She recalled the camaraderie she felt when she began talking to Jennifer. "We're going to the same conference," she remembered saying, flashing a presenters' package identical to the one her aisle mate examined. "Do you mind talking shop?"

"Not at all. What's your presentation about?"

"Sustainable community," Marva said. "Yours?"

"Greening multinational developers."

Marva grunted. "You mean you only plan to talk for three minutes?"

"We could trade horror stories about developers for hours. I'd prefer to swap strategies for working with them," Jennifer said.

The two women cackled loudly and often in between listening to each other's success stories. They put the armrest between them up and huddled together like little girls playing jacks on a narrow, stone step.

"Girl, some folks call me the witch of the West. But my Momma named me Marva," she said, extending her hand. "You're clearly the me of the East. A joy to meet you."

Their conversation moved from work to dreams. Both women were planning to begin their families within the year. Both worried out loud about how to help their children become self-loving, Life-revering adults.

"My only fear is of being ineffective against prejudices they'll pick up from their teachers and playmates," Jennifer said. "Personally, I don't see color."

I hope your disability isn't genetic, Marva thought. She felt her interest in developing their relationship fading as she imagined the melanin in her skin fading into—what? What is the color of just humans? She breathed deeply to keep an accelerating thumpthumping in her stomach from migrating into her throat. In a voice almost free of sharp edges she said, "I know you probably mean well, but . . ."

"I need to stretch out," Marva said as soon as the captain stopped talking.

The DC-10's long aisles were perfect for a show. Marva's dress caressed her arms in fuchsia waves of silk as she slipped into her power walk: pelvis tilted slightly forward, shoulders held slightly back, hips and legs swiveling from side to side as required to maintain her gravity-defying angle. Her expression—detached, self-contained, part of the posture. She savored the men's obvious desire, the women's jealous approval; energy her body registered as the next best nourishment to being touched.

And she so needed to be touched, rocked, cuddled—given some kind of fortifying attention—if the wet in Jennifer's eyes meant what it typically did in the eyes of white people who, barely knowing her, spoke to Marva of their inability to see color: this woman with whom she was destined to spend the next seventeen hours traveling to New Zealand was filled to spilling out with some Black story.

Marva always traveled with herbs for the last nerve such people inevitably got on. They never quite looked Marva in the eye as they battered her ears with tales of color-coded pain. As soon as they got what Marva led them to believe was a sympathetic hearing, they'd leave without so much as a thank you ma'am.

Frequently, Marva attracted stories from white people raised to rein in their expression of love for the Black women who mothered them, women who were said to be but not treated just like one of the family. Marva was baffled by the number of such people she met in her travels. Was it her karma or something she did or didn't eat? Should she add more garlic to her diet?

"Life, help," Marva prayed softly as she walked, addressing the elements like her mother addressed the Lord. "When I just think about white women's Black stories, my jaws get tight."

"Count the blessings of this mess," Life answered, in her mother's voice.

"Open mine eyes that I may see," Marva said.

She swiveled past several washrooms into the one closest to the tail, splashed cold water on her face. Was this her fate or what? Here she was, the only Black woman on a flight with every one of its four hundred seats filled, and she gets the one next to a gushing storyholder.

Hatred; hatred and the violent poverty her education and mother's love helped her escape were the only things she hated worse than white people's insistence on telling her their Black stories. Marva pondered her violent physical reaction to news of Jennifer's disability. She felt like a hypocrite, impoverished by the scarcity of Black women, men, children, and elders in the otherwise natural environments she worked so hard to sustain.

"Looka here, Life, if sending me these folks with their Black stories is your way of saying ain't no hiding place, I got it," Marva said.

She reminded Life that she hadn't completely abandoned the neighborhood of her youth. She gave talks at schools, helped out in whatever ways her mother said to during her quarterly visits. And while Marva's nerves could stand only a week or two of the neighborhood she'd endured law school to escape, she gave thanks for the juice of her visits.

Where else could she find so many women who knew and had lovingly touched her since she was no higher than their close-to-the-ground knees? Who else but all her Mommas and Aunties up and down the street called her baby in voices that sounded like different shades of velvet? Something about the way those Black women loved fortified her for months.

The washroom became a much-needed sanctuary for which Marva gave thanks. She called on memories of home's magic to keep her company. She hadn't noticed being outnumbered 399 to 1 until Jennifer's declaration gave her the choice of either drowning or walking past row after row of babbling, coughing, drinking, sleeping, grinning, vacant, nonblack faces. Marva imagined approaching the head flight attendant to arrange a bit of in-flight entertainment, tailored to her captive audience's demographics.

Ladies and gentlemen, may I have your attention? We're pleased to offer you a special treat today, courtesy of Dr. Marva Freewyn, world-renowned color therapist. Thank you, Kim, Dr. Freewyn says in her CNN voice. Let's begin by taking a simple poll. How many of you have Black stories—challenging relationships with or haunting memories of Black people? (Nearly half of the passengers raise their hands.) How many of you have told these stories to your white colleagues, friends, relations, or therapists? (All but five hands slowly forsake the air.) How many long to unburden your soul's dark tales into some Black person's ears? (Far too many for me to accommodate and still have time to nap, eat, and see the movie before landing.)

In an attempt to devise a fair system for handling your over-whelming demand, I'll listen to the first six people willing to pay ten thousand dollars for the privilege of telling me their Black story. Indicate your interest by pushing the flight attendant call button. (The response sounds like someone got lucky at a slot machine.) While the attendants take your names, seat numbers, and traveler's checks—made out to the National Black Story Catcher's Project—let me tell you about the training program your fees will support.

Our program helps Black women develop facial expressions, mannerisms, vocabulary, personal style, concerned curiosity, and empathetic skills nine out of ten people just like you say are most helpful in drawing out their Black stories. What's more, we teach our students self-care techniques—including pacing, maintaining their identities, and deftly attending to their own emotional needs while serving as impersonal backdrops for your memories—so that your collective tendency to tell and run in total disregard of your listeners' humanity doesn't prematurely shorten their years of cheerful service. Finally, we show them how to socialize their daughters from birth to perfect the same skills.

Marva gave herself the gift of as much guilt-free solitude as needed to regain her composure. She asked Life for guidance.

"You've only got to move a little further down this road," Life answered.

Encouraged, Marva began her story-catching pep talk: That's right, girl, you've almost got this one licked. Remember, just last week, when the old white man telling you how to reassemble a table he'd taken apart to fit into your car was interrupted by his wife's saying,

"You don't have to tell a Black girl how to do that. Black girls know all about that stuff."

Marva's pause was no longer than the inhale it took her to respond, "Not all Black *women* are alike. I'm happy to get his instruction."

"Well, I just came back from visiting a Black girl I know in Florida. She's seventy-two. I love her. She knows a lot."

"Oh," Marva said, consciously working to make her jaws relax, "you're talking about an *elder*, someone older than you. Different old Black women know different things."

It was a practically pain-free teachable moment.

"All right, Life, maybe I'll have this one down by the time I'm seventy-two," Marva said. "Thanks a bunch for the assignment of uplifting the race by neutralizing yet another storyholder."

Somebody had to, she thought, or else the storyholders' pain would color their hiring decisions, tinge their institutions, spatter their children and their children's children and her children and on and on.

She tried to anticipate the theme of Jennifer's story: I wish *more* of you could afford to be here. (Response #1: But I'm the only one of me there is. Response #2: It's not a matter of money. Response #3: You have my ears, what *more* of me do you want?) I had a Black friend once. Black people aren't friendly to me on the streets; can you tell me why? I understand what it means to be Black because I have a Black lover. I thought I understood what it meant to be Black until my Black lover almost killed me. I had a son by a Black man, and I don't know how to raise him; help me. Black people are prejudiced, too. I chose to transfer out of the school into which Black kids were being bused, and I feel guilty about it because I want us to be friends. Will you forgive me?

Marva returned to her seat. She placed and adjusted one pillow behind her back, another behind her neck. Sighed. Wished for a pacifying slice of her mother's sweet potato pie.

As soon as Marva turned to meet Jennifer's eyes, Jennifer started explaining, "When we first talked we seemed compatible enough to someday be friends. I was afraid you wouldn't be interested in more than a professional relationship if I didn't say something to prove I'm different than most well-intentioned white Americans."

Keep talking, Marva thought. She told Jennifer, "I'm listening."

"What I meant to say is that I try to respect everyone, no matter what the color of their skin."

Some of Marva felt partially responsible for the pinch she saw in Jennifer's face. Most of her didn't. Another part whispered, "Stop acting what your Momma would call ugly." She ignored it.

"So what do you want from me?" Marva asked. "If I charged for the gazillion times white folks have pressed me into being their confessor, I could afford to fly first class the rest of my life."

"I don't want to press you into anything," Jennifer said. "We're on the same side, remember?"

"You want to be on my side?" Marva asked. "See color."

She slowly stroked her fuchsia sleeves back, raised her cherry-wood arms—as though she were conducting an orchestra or about to perform magic—and caressed them, reveling in the skin it had taken her two forevers to stop hating. Jennifer made the same click-ing sound, the sound of a match being struck, that Marva's mother always made right before saying, "Chile, stop your foolishness."

"Spare me your dramatics," Jennifer said.

Marva's hands raced to her hips.

"Spare me your denials," she said. "I wish you'd checked your projections with your baggage before getting on this plane. Admit it, my skin reminds you of some*colored*body else you haven't been able to get or forget."

"Yes and no—since *you* insist on having this conversation," Jennifer said. "Yes, before you got so perturbed you reminded me of the Black woman who mothered me; you have her eyes. And no, I will never forget her. Never."

Marva started rocking, tending to her own comfort, humming so softly that only she could hear it.

"Was she my color?" Marva asked.

"Just about," Jennifer said. "She had an accepting way of looking at people. Her name was Vera; Vera Ginger."

Jesus, I really could create a training program, Marva thought, to wit: To gauge and therefore prepare for the weight of projections you're about to bear, ask tellers of *I Had a Black Nanny* stories, "Is she still alive?"

"No, she died two years ago. I was out of the country when it happened. By the time my parents finally got through to me she was already buried." Jennifer's eyes were awash again.

Something warm ached and grew concentrically in the middle of Marva's chest. She saw her own mother, seventy-five and still gettin' up but seventy-five ain't young and how would I feel if something happened to her while I'm flying over this ocean? Offering what comfort she honestly could, Marva began humming loudly enough for Jennifer to hear.

"People called her Mother Ginger. And called her and called her. She'd interpret their dreams, help them solve their problems at any hour of the day or night. Vera was always reading the Bible."

If she'd been listening to a Black woman telling this story about her real mother, Marva would have offered to hold her hand.

"Vera taught me to count and give thanks for my blessings three times a day," Jennifer said. "I learned how to cook by helping her. I helped her as often as I could. My other mother did her best to make sure I didn't forget my place. But she couldn't stop me from climbing into Vera's lap and touching her skin."

(Have mercy havemercy. Your mother paid a Momma like mine to be yours.) The warm throbbing down into Marva's stomach softened the little bit of fight she struggled to retain just in case more race mess rushed out of Jennifer's mouth. Marva caressed her own cheek.

"I loved touching Vera's face, just like you're touching yours now," Jennifer said. "She taught me that respecting all of life was the answer to everything. I keep trying to figure out how to live in a way that makes her right."

"So Life, you and Momma Ginger sent me to do this work with Jennifer, didn't you?" Marva asked under her breath. "All right then. It's you and me, Momma G. If I talk to your little Jenny like you would, long enough, while stroking my face, I suspect she'll heal a little and stop calling on you so much. That means you'll get some rest.

"If it works, will you and Life *paleeze* relieve me of this second-hand Mammyhood?"

of theretime
in heretime

HARRIET TUBMAN

how many miles did you go without eating
or eating, fast, foods what grew wild

how did you know what was nourishing
which way was safe
how deeply to wade in the water

waking from your place of slaving for others
you walked into freedom
for how many hundreds of miles
hundreds of miles = how many days on foot

Elder Harriet Tubman
how did you keep your self North
nights when clouds sheltered the stars

tell us the *natchel* of nature, the freedom of being you knew
water and critters and woodlands to be

you knew Life well and lived by it
Harriet Tubman
tell us your secrets, please

IN THE CHRISTIAN LAND that I made my own by foot, wheel, boat, horse, by star and moss's preference for North, I was called Moses because I kept coming back to help free other people. Buddhists would call me a bodhisattva. I lived my vows. I called what guided me God. I listened. Frederick Douglass said my valor was witnessed by the silent stars.

Poor Frederick. Though we were slaves in the same country, I didn't know he didn't have the ears to hear the stars singing. So many times, more times than I can shake a stick at, stars' songs guided me and the people who dared to come with me all the way home.

Sure, some folks got afraid. Them, I gave the choice: go forward or die. I carried shotguns sometimes, but my favorite weapon was a pistol. I wasn't 'fraid of death, saw plenty blood. I never lost a passenger, and I never took one's life, but I sho' was willing to. The white folks called my actions audacity. I have them to thank in a way. I played their delusions of superiority all up in their faces; *natchel.*

Take, for instance, my hearing tell that my seventy-year-old father was accused of doing something that could get him hurt bad. Clear as a bell, what I heard told me it was time to steal my parents into freedom, whether they were ready or not. I needed twenty dollars for the trip and went to the antislavery office in Philly to get it, just like my inner voice told me to do. The man in the office asked me who told me to come and get twenty dollars from him.

"My God told me," I said.

"Well, your God was wrong," the man retorted. "You'll not get twenty dollars from me."

"My God ain't been wrong yet," I informed my reluctant benefactor. "I'm going to set right here as long as it takes for me to get my twenty dollars."

Down I sat and went into one of my sleeps. When I woke up some time later there was sixty dollars in my lap. With that I went to steal my folks free. Went into their master's stable and hitched one of their master's horses up to one of their master's buggies and rode us all into town.

What could be more natural than a wagon filled with three old slavish-looking people calmly riding into town on a errand for they master? What other reason could we possibly have for riding into town? When you assume your inferiors can't think a thought or raise a finger unless you say so, you less likely to question their very questionable presence, so secure you become in your rule.

I counted on such foolishness. My ugliness, my hunched-over shuffle, my sleeping "sickness," all tools. Not that I'm calling anybody fools, na-ahh. I just made the most of what I was given: a voice to sing out the signals of freedom leaving under cover of night, a powerful practice of praying for guidance and acting on what I heard. Look at my ears in those pictures of me. Notice how prominent they are, flowering on the side of my head. Those with eyes to see could tell how important my ears were.

Whoever saw me with my parents in town that day musta just knowed we were there on proper business. How could we otherwise be so bold? This is what I mean when I say I counted on bigotry.

Bless bigotry's blindness.

In and out of town we rode, just as nice, then up North to freedom. My parents, full-blooded Asanti, birthed me into slavery. I delivered them their liberty. Sometimes what goes around comes back 'round better.

Ask your daughter.

*We
who
create
what is
coming*

I S THERE SOME WORD or phrase, descriptive of some quality of
being, that you are ready to more fully live?
Bring your voice to those longed-for qualities of Life. If you feel
something tickling the back of your throat, it already has you; perhaps it's a chant.

What if your longing to live certain songs echoes a longing of Life
for your voice? What if your answering Life's calls to sound will
help our entire species come 'round to restorative living?

Begin simply to bring what you hear to your lips. One note is
tone enough for many birds. Perhaps if you walk down the street
with a friend, singing, singing at a pace that could be conversation
but chanting, at the pace and volume of conversation, no one would
know. Perhaps they would think it was somebody's radio, or be so
accustomed to unhearing ambient sound that the two of you could
pass unhindered moments in pedestrian sound.

Begin simply. Begin by extending one word in an otherwise normal conversation. Begin by singing yes, then saying we'd love to
host your three daughters in our shop on "Take Your Daughters to
Work" day.

Begin more simply still. Begin by being quiet and still, still enough
to feel your heart beating under your hand-skin touching your own
chest-skin. Begin as close as possible to being as naked as the day
before you were born, naked in all of your senses. Quietly, curl up
into a fetal position and feel the pulsing of your cells. Notice if there

are differences between pulses felt in different spots on your body. Resist, if possible, the temptation to understand the different pulsings. (Are the apparent differences between pulses aural allusions? Are they the forerunners of what recording engineers call reverb and delay?)

Resist analysis. Appreciate each pulsing. Acknowledge your effortlessly polyrhythmic being. Then, focusing on the pulse felt under your hand when you touch your chest, sing-say *I am e-nough,* one word per heartbeat.

No trees, no oxygen. No oxygen, no fresh breath to energize cells through the blood's caress. No vitalized blood with which to replace blood filled with waste, no job for the heart, no food for the rest of the organs. No new air, no Life for us. Our living is miraculous. Begin simply by touching your heart with a deeply felt humm.

Try a deep hum every other heartbeat. Make it a hum you can feel clear down to your feet. Remember the humming that comes with an insight. Remember the humming of being well fed. Remember the humming of deeply loving another, of generosity given or received.

Attend free, open-air concerts (live!) in a mixed conifer forest blown through by winds. Match your breathing to a young pine tree's swaying. Then give the length of each out-breath a tone. Begin your tone with a humming that vibrates the bones of your face and neck. Finding that tone will take pecking around a bit, trying first one note and then one higher or lower. Do this in patience and solitude or with a trusted, also experimenting, friend. But stay with the tone that allows you to feel your breath's resonant, full-bodied dimensions. Then hum that tone again and again.

What is the tone of beliefs and intentions to which you devote your breath every day? What relationships exist between your body's rhythms—the pulsing of adrenaline, the holding of your breath—and the thoughts cycling around and around in your mind's ear? What are the chants of your Life time?

Begin again. Japa, divine daughters. Repeat the phrase *divine daughters* each time you move your feet. Assign divinity your left foot today. Tomorrow, see how divine your right foot feels. Step left (divine) then right (daughters) slowly across your kitchen floor. Walking down the hall to the women's room, step left (daughters) then right (divine).

Japa. Chant. Each over and over we enter has been breathed by others billions of times before. A kinship exists between twinkle, twinkle, little star, and the chants we birthed at Gaia, having fun, la-la-la. Our praisesongs of fluid, sonorous bodies, of Yemaya's and of our own—full chants. Chants: born of sorrow and gratitude. Chants: born of mystery. Chants: born of work to be done and joy.

Step into Life's everywhere, always streaming music.
Sing and live what you hear.

GLOSSARY

ayah: A wetnurse or nursemaid in Hindu society. A member of the milkman cast.

betchu: Bet you; a wager.

bhakti: Loving devotion: a spiritual path that flowered into a popular movement throughout India in medieval times.

bioregion: An ecologically centered method for locating place. Bioregions are organized around watersheds rather than political designations.

Daddytongue: Language learned orally from Daddy's everyday speech.

daymare: Daytime nightmares. A frightening daydream often accompanied by sensations of oppression and helplessness.

Earthma: Term of endearment for the planet Earth.

Earthwide: Extending throughout the Earth.

essensual: essential sensual nature of something.

godblamed: Strongly cursed or blamed.

gottu: Got to.

heroinic: A courageous act of a heroine.

ism: A system, theory, doctrine, etc., especially one whose name ends in *-ism*.

Japa: Mantric repetition. A mantra is empowered or spiritual speech.

jougging: getting on someone's last nerve.

juxed: Slang for *juxtaposed*. Coined by author.

Kali: Hindu goddess. Goddess as the powers of transformation and death.

kinfolks: Relatives. Used to designate relatives of blood and extended family.

koan: In Zen Buddhism, a question asked of a student to bring the student through contemplation of it to greater awareness of reality.

lingam: A ritual designation of a phallus or phallic symbol in Hindu religion.

Loa: A deity in Vodoun religious practices.

matrilineal: Associated with the kinship systems and associated customs in which people trace their descent and inheritance through a female line and female ancestors. Approximately one-third of the world's societies are considered matrilineal.

matrilocal: A common residence practice and system in the world where a young couple lives with or near the bride's parents or family members after their wedding. Matrilocal may also mean the home territory of the matrilineal tribe.

Mommaline: Matrilineal ancestry or matriline.

Mommatongue: Language learned orally from Momma's everyday speech.

moontime: A woman's bleeding time: menstruation.

numinous: Having a deeply spiritual or mystical effect.

Petro: Usually used in association with *Loa*. A Petro Loa is a wrathful Vodoun deity.

polyrhythms: Strongly contrasting rhythms in simultaneous voice parts.

praisesongs: Traditionally, a form of poetry in African oral traditions that extols the feats and personal qualities of the rulers.

rememories: The plural of *rememory*, a term coined by Toni Morrison to mean a reevaluation of memories or even a reconstruction of the memory to shed a more bearable light on past experiences and legacies.

restory: To restore soul and spirit with the use of stories. Replacing oppressive cultural myths with ones that affirm one's being.

riff: Improvise.

sadiddy: Uppity; snobbish and pretentious.

spiritkin: Relatives related by spiritual practices, understandings, and beliefs.

thrival: *Thrival* is to *thrive* as *survival* is to *survive*.

whatchu: What you.

wildcraft: To gather one's medicines, herbs, berries, roots, tree bark, etc., from the wild.

FOR FURTHER READING

The following writings have all been helpful in the ongoing research on divine daughters. Books written for young readers are marked with an *.

Allen, Paula Gunn. Grandmothers of the Light—A Medicine Woman's Sourcebook. Boston: Beacon Press, 1991.

Allione, Tsultrim. Women of Wisdom. London: Routledge & Kegan Paul, 1984.

Altman, Meryl. "How Not To Do Things With Metaphors We Live By." College English, September 1990: Vol. 52, No. 5, pp. 495–506.

Ann, Martha and Dorothy Myers Imel. Goddesses in World Mythology. New York: Oxford University Press, Inc., 1993.

Asram, Saradeswari. Gauri Mata. Calcutta: Durga Puri Devi, 1944.

Barnstone, Aliki and Willis, eds. A Book of Women Poets—From Antiquity to Now. New York: Schocken Books, Inc., 1992.

Brenner, Athalya, ed. A Feminist Companion to Exodus to Deuteronomy. England: Sheffield Academic Press, 1994.

Bronner, Leila Leah. From Eve to Esther—Rabbinic Reconstructions of Biblical Women. Louisville: Westminster/John Knox Press, 1994.

Chipasula, Frank and Stella, eds. The Heinemann book of African Women's Poetry. Oxford: Heinemann Educational Publishers, 1995.

Cleary, Thomas, ed. Immortal Sisters—Secrets of Taoist Women. Boston: Shambhala Publications, Inc., 1989.

Cooey, Paula, William R. Eakin and Jay B. McDaniel, eds. After Patriarchy—Feminist Transformations of the World Religions. New York: Orbis Books, 1991.

Cott, Jonathan, ed. Skies in Blossom—The Nature Poetry of Emily Dickinson. New York: Doubleday, 1995.

Deen, Edith. All of the Women of the Bible. New York: Harper Brothers Publishers, 1955.

Doriani, Beth Maclay. Emily Dickinson, Daughter of Prophecy. Amherst: The University of Massachusetts Press, 1996.

Drake, William. The First Wave—Women Poets in America 1915–1945. New York: Collier Books, Macmillan Publishing Company, 1987.

Estés, Clarissa Pinkola, Ph.D. Women Who Run With the Wolves—Myths and Stories of the Wild Woman Archetype. New York: Ballantine Books, 1995.

Frankel, Ellen, Ph.D. The Five Books of Miriam. New York: Crossett/Putnam, 1996.

Freedman, David Noel. The Anchor Bible Dictionary. New York: Doubleday, 1992.

Frisbie, Charlotte Johnson. Kinaaldá—A Study of the Navaho Girl's Puberty Ceremony. Salt Lake City: University of Utah Press, 1993.

*Hamilton, Virginia. (Illustrations by Leo and Diane Dillon). Her Stories—African American Folktales, Fairy Tales, and True Tales. New York: The Blue Sky Press, 1995.

Hawley, John Stratton and Donna Marie Wulff, eds. Devi—Goddesses of India. Berkeley: University of California Press, 1996.

Hawley, John Stratton and Donna Marie Wulff, eds. The Divine Consort—Radha and the Goddess of India. Berkeley: Graduate Theological Union, 1982.

Heilbrun, Carolyn G. Writing a Woman's Life. New York: Ballantine Books, 1988.

Hirshfield, Jane. Women in Praise of the Sacred—43 Centuries of Spiritual Poetry by Women. New York: HarperCollins Publishers, Inc., 1994.

*Hopkinson, Deborah (paintings by James Ransome). Sweet Clara and the Freedom Quilt. New York: Alfred A. Knopf, Inc., 1993.

Ishtar, Zohl Dé. Daughters of the Pacific. Australia: Spinifex Press, 1994.

Johnson, Linda. Daughters of the Goddess—The Women Saints of India. St. Paul: Yes International Publishers, 1995.

Madhavananda, Swami and Ramesh Chandra Majumdar, eds. Great

Women of India. Himalayas: Swami Gambhirananda, 1953.

Meyers, Carol. Discovering Eve—Ancient Israelite Women in Context. New York: Oxford University Press, Inc., 1988.

Molinaro, Ursule. A Full Moon of Women. New York: Penguin Group, 1990.

Murcott, Susan. The First Buddhist Women—Translations and Commentary on the Therigatha. Berkeley: Parallax Press, 1991.

Newsom, Carol and Sharon Ringe, eds. The Women's Bible Commentary. Louisville: Westminster/John Knox Press, 1992.

Painter, Nell Irvin. Sojourner Truth—A Life, a Symbol. New York: W. W. Norton & Co., Inc., 1996.

Reagon, Bernice Johnson and Sweet Honey in the Rock. Sweet Honey in the Rock . . . Still on the Journey. New York: Doubleday, 1993.

Sakenfeld, Katharine Doob. "Feminist Biblical Interpretation." Theology Today, July 1989: Vol. 46, No. 2, pp. 154–164.

Sered, Susan Starr. Pristess, Mother, Sacre Sisster-Religions Dominated by Women. New York: Oxford University Press, Inc., 1994.

Sertima, Ivan Van, ed. Black Women in Antiquity. New Brunswick: Transaction Publishers, 1992.

Shaw, Miranda. Passionate Enlightenment—Women in Tantric Buddhism. New Jersey: Princeton University Press, 1994.

Silverblatt, Irene Marsha. Moon, Sun, and Devil: Inca and Colonial Transformations of Andean Gender Relations (Volumes 1 and 2). Michigan: UMI, 1981.

Stone, Merlin. Ancient Mirrors of Womanhood—A Treasury of Goddess and Heroine Lore from Around the World. Boston: Beacon Press, 1984.

Taylor, M. W. Harriet Tubman. New York: Chelsea House Publishers, 1991.

Williams, Terry Tempest and Mary Frank. Desert Quartet. New York: Pantheon Books, 1995.

ACKNOWLEDGMENTS

Where does the sung come from?
My heartful gratitude to the valleys of Vallecitos and the river that runs through them. Thank you, Linda Velarde and Grove Burnett, for protecting this sanctuary.

Momma, Daddy, and Nelson, our lifetime of loving, growing, praying, laughing, fussing, singing, and forgiving together is music to my soul. I feel blessed to belong to our family. Many Mommas introduced me to the trials and triumphs of belonging to spirited vocal communities and extended families. Among them, I give special thanks to Mrs. Audrey Fletcher, Momma Jones, Momma Ginger, Mom Jenkins, Mrs. Norris, Miss Carey, Miss Vera, Mrs. Bivens, and Miss Rose.

All praises to the women beside whom I've come home to the drum: Linda Tillery, Tynowyn, Barbara Borden, and Layne Redmond.

Daughter Sister communities, thank you for your welcoming ears:
Women of the Bay Area and National Black Women's Health Project, particularly Felicia Ward and Byllye Avery, your mountainous loving brought me back to Life in the sisterhood of Africa's daughters. May the healing you make possible for so many others bless you.

Women of the WomanEarth Feminist Peace Institute, we walked a ways together. The work we began with one another continues.

Women of Women's Alliance Camps, led by Charlotte Kelly, offered so many of us a context in which to practice creating together. I am grateful for the continuing friendships we planted in our campgrounds.

Women of Color as Warriors of Lights, born of Carmen Freeman's vision, may the elder and younger daughters that gather together each year continue to shine, shine, shine.

Elders, teachers, sisters, and brothers of growing things, thank you for helping me be true to Life's music: Momma, Deb Soule, JoAnn Liddell, JoAnne O'Neil, Rosemary Gladstar, Alexander Johnston, Susan Root, Rosita Arvigo, Miss Hortense Robinson, Mark Cohen, Amy

Lohman, Andrea and Matthias Risen, Diane DeLuca, Louise Lacey, James Duke, and Debbie Chapman.

Louise, thank you for your pioneering work in "Lunaception" and your newsletters, *Women's Choice* and *Growing Native.*

Teachers, friends, and colleagues at the nexus of the pen and public action: Toni Morrison, Grace Paley, Linda Hogan, David Abram, Deena Metzger, Robert Hass, the writers and artists of the Watershed conference, Denise Levertov, Charlene Spretnak, Starhawk, Luisah Teish, Elena Featherston, Fran Peavey, Christina Baldwin, Daphne Muse, August Wilson; Terry Tempest Williams, Alice Walker, and Clarissa Pinkola Estés; thank you all for the luminous examples your lives are.

Members of the "Hanover Nascence" writing group, in which the bits and pieces that finally shaped themselves into *Divine Daughters* first saw the light of day: Judy Byfield, Martin Davidson, Deborah King, Patrick Nicoletti, and Dee Royster. You were outrageous comadres and copadres.

Dreaming, editing, and imaging buddies extraordinaire: Beth Arnold, S. Michael Bessie, Gail Baker, Christina Baldwin, Rachael Cohen, Inja Ink, Colleen Kelly, and Daphne Muse. Each of you brought an essential eye and ear to the elephantine task of writing the life that eventually became *Divine Daughters.* All praises.

Infinite gratitude to my mentors, champions, and Stanford family: Jack Daniels, Ladoris Cordell, Shirley Wedlake, Jack Friedenthal, Karen Cook, and Jerusha Stewart, you were my lights and my way when I returned to Stanford Law School. Jim Cadena, you called so many voices out of me, *thank you.* Aleta Hayes, when we dance, the universe dances. Kennell Jackson, African and Afro-American Studies, Faye McNair, Annayalea Middleton, The Black House, Sandra Richardson, Black Performing Arts, Halifu Osumare, Sylvia Wynter, St. Claire Drake, the Martin Luther King, Jr., Papers Project crew, Mary Dillard, Marshelle Jones, Mary Hayes, Kathy Namphy, Ujamanians, Floyd Thompkins: you all left your voiceprints on my bones. Many, many thanks.

Ysaye Barnwell, Linda Tillery and the Cultural Heritage Choir, Bobby McFerrin, the Stras—Kirsten Falk, Sara Jennison, Raz Kennedy,

Joey Blake, Nick Bearde, David Worm, Molly Holm, Linda Tillery, Rhiannon—sisters of the SisterSingers Network, Cathy Roma, Victoria Christgau, and Caprice Fox: I continue to learn from our vocal sojourns.

Many thanks to the Squaw Valley Community of Writers, especially Lucille Clifton, for lending your voices to the births of poems in *Divine Daughters*. Many thanks to David Fuqua of Highland Music Engraving for your ears and exacting music transcriptions.

Constance Bellavance, Joy and George Langford, Tanielle McBain: your transcription, research, and administrative skills continually breathed life into my work.

Francés J. Jones, Ned Hearn, Ned Leavitt, California Lawyers for the Arts, Alma Robinson, and the National Writers' Union: thank you for helping me navigate the frequently troubled waters of creative "industries."

Caroline Pincus, your midwifery of *Divine Daughters* was stellar. To all of you at Harper San Francisco who extended yourselves to bring *Divine Daughters* through the storm—many, many thanks.

All praises for your life-sustaining, culinary ministrations: Jeanne and Tonito Matos and Jennifer Le Mieux.

And endless gratitude to Martin Davidson, for being the closest the longest. You continue to teach me just how careful we need to be in the past.

ABOUT THE AUTHOR

Rachel Bagby, J.D., began teaching creativity programs for daughters at the age of fifteen. A graduate of Stanford Law School, she writes about relationships between nature and culture, and her work has appeared in many anthologies and periodicals, including *Essence, Ms.,* the *Wall Street Journal,* and *Time.* For four years she performed with Bobby McFerrin's Voicestra. Her voice and compositions are featured in several documentaries, including the Emmy Award–winning documentary *Dialogues with Madwomen* and *Alice Walker: Visions of the Spirit.* Music from her recording label, outta the box, and music publishing company, Breathing Music, is broadcast and performed worldwide.

Visit *Divine Daughters'* website: www.divinedaughters.com